William Benjamin Philpot

A Pocket of Pebbles, with a Few Shells

Being fragments of reflection, now and then with cadence, made up mostly by the

sea-shore

William Benjamin Philpot

A Pocket of Pebbles, with a Few Shells
Being fragments of reflection, now and then with cadence, made up mostly by the sea-shore

ISBN/EAN: 9783337378042

Printed in Europe, USA, Canada, Australia, Japan

Cover: Foto ©Andreas Hilbeck / pixelio.de

More available books at **www.hansebooks.com**

A Pocket of Pebbles,

WITH A FEW SHELLS;

BEING

FRAGMENTS OF REFLECTION,

NOW AND THEN WITH ?

CADENCE,

MADE UP MOSTLY BY THE SEA-SHORE.

BY

WILLIAM PHILPOT,

VICAR IN THE HOLY ORDERS OF THE ·CHURCH
OF CHRIST AND OF ENGLAND.

[RIGHTS OF TRANSLATION RESERVED.]

LONDON:
MACMILLAN AND CO.,
1877.

DEDICATED

TO

THE WORLD AND—MY WIFE.

Preface.

"THESE are but pelting matters," some may opine; and for my own part, in exposing the contents of my satchel, I hardly know what I ought to say, and what I ought not. And yet, besides the having to say something, I feel as if, by way of preface, I had something to say. Such an introduction to a book is much as when a man in making a speech begins *sotto voce*, partly that he may gauge the pitch of the building, and partly that he may break upon his audience less loudly and rudely. Those who do not want a preface, will not read it; and those who will read it may be presumed to have wanted it.

If I am called to account for this 'litel boke,' it might be enough in these days to say that a man may well court the ranks of publicity as a refuge from the reproach of singularity. But to those who may not regard this reason as ample, and who may care to ask of me further, I may say that the cause, not of these "pebbles" being gathered and pocketed—for that had been a private and harmless fancy already foregone—but of their being offered to my neighbours, was simply on this wise.

Not long ago, a worthy friend, whose praise is in the presses, urged me to put some of my thinkings together. Now, to be garrulous for a moment, be it known to all men by these presents, that the aforesaid friend is among those genial men to whom you cannot but listen. He is one whom, in his rare leisure, nothing delights more than to take the treasures which he has found among the worm-eaten caskets of our half-forgotten poets, and because it pitieth him to see them in the dust, to lift them up again to the light, and, preserving with loving care all their ancient touches, newly to set them. And this it was, I am free to confess, more than anything else, which drew me and won me to listen to the request which he saw fit to urge. For I could not but secretly feel, that if ever, among those thinkers to whom may safely be applied the words "advanced" and "high," I should live to look for more precious stones than these along the beaches of any Island of the Blest—and if ever a man of so kindly a soul, in the days that are coming, should in like manner bethink him to bring back to the day anything which he might find me, for my poor part, to have gathered upon the low shores of the sweet world—I felt, I say, that in such an hour my light organism, in remembrance of this pleasing, anxious being, would surely tingle again with such pleasure as the circumstances might permit. So sitting with him among his rare collection of venerable editions, and his pleasant pictures, the walls of my life-long reserve fell at the third winding of his desire. Thus it was, to make my story short, that, over-pressed in perhaps an unlucky moment, I revealed to him that I happened to have a heap of old pocket-books, and said that I would sift them over to see if I could thus comply with his wish.

I am well aware that what I have advanced would serve me but ill as an excuse for foisting on the public any ideas which might not be deemed worthy of them; but as in the course of my quest I came again upon these random pencillings, some after many years, almost with the mind and eye of a stranger, and found that for me they still held true and had some interest, I thought they might perchance interest others, if once they were set for them in readable type. However, such as they are, here they

are. Here is my little bag of fragmentary reflections, picked up with many others along my
special humanity in short walks beside the eternal sea of Thought and Fancy, and most of
them dropped into my pocket in broken turns,
taken amidst laborious work, beside our English
Channel that washes this pleasant coast to which
my well-beloved Primate has sent me.

As to the form. Though the omen may not
be happy, I meant my little stones for bread :—
and it seemed better to minister this in morsels.
Sermons, if seldom, as they say, listened to, are,
I learn, still more rarely read. He that can get
through some of our sermons is like that Neapol-
itan who swallowed 60 yards of macaroni without a break, a feat to which I could not expect
many of my readers would be equal. My Tutor
had a merry jest about a Very Reverend uncle of
his, whose dutiful niece passed part of her Sunday
evenings in reading to him discourses of the old
divines. Of this he would bear a little ; but when
she heard s(o)norous cadences coming from beneath the silken kerchief which veiled that
prophet of Bangor, she would fall into a *minu-
endo*, in due time come to a pause, and, drawing a dial from her poke, pursue fancy-free her
maiden meditations. When time duly warned,

she would very wisely recommence in an exquisite *crescendo*, and so close that sermon. Awaking with a start, and hearing the silence, the Dean would exclaim "Admirable discourse! let us have another;" upon which the manner of the performance would be resumed *Da Capo al Segno*, and so *al Fine*. I thought therefore I would meet this excellent device by the cruel stratagem of enforced pauses; so that, if any slumberous hearer should look for sermons in pebbles, some fair reader might keep him awake by a *staccato* ministration of something short, perhaps crisp, at least disconnected.

I refrain from quoting the well-known authorities for this form which I have chosen, lest I should seem to aim at keeping pace with those whom, *non passibus aequis*, I only strive to follow. How the thoughts of those great men fell into those immortal crystals I can but guess. I presume every one, who loves to cull and study the words of the wise, fills his own mind, of whatever calibre, with forms into which naturally fall the best gatherings his wealth or his poverty can provide from his expatiations with himself on the solitary sand of thought.

As to the name. "Aphorisms" seemed too grand a title, and one more befitting the utterances of those who have acquired fame enough to demand a general hearing, and to impart prestige to their sententiousness. But I thought I might fairly, without any offence or semblance of presumption, style these *collectanea* of my own reflections "a pocket of pebbles":—a name which, if you will bear with me, may be shown to carry its small conceits. Pebbles are picked up in walks by shores : so were most of these. Pebbles are chips of more or less interest struck off by unknown agency : so are these, rounded as they are by the roll and wash of the times and tides of the soul. Pebbles vary in size : so do these. Pebbles are hard little things : so may some of these be considered, by those who have not yet had the mental or perhaps spiritual sensibilities so exercised as inwardly to digest them. Pebbles are found to hit hard, if aimed well and thrown straight : so it may be, I hope, with some of these : but that is for those to say who may feel them ! Pebbles vary in value : so do these. If *all* these pieces of thought and observation were *very* wise, my readers might grow weary of wisdom. As it is, the lighter ones may perhaps serve to digest the heavier. Again, in some pebbles, a kindly use of the tongue shows something precious—perhaps a riband of that fortification which, as children, we thought so much of in our agates. On the other hand, there are some which no expenditure of lingual aid can show to be worth our keeping; for when the momentary and adventitious shine is off, and the factitious splendour past away, they fade into the dulness of common flint! So, alas, it may be with too many of mine; and I can only say that, where this is shown to me, such shall forthwith be flipped back again into the sea from which the idle waves have washed them. Yet some pebbles, and I hope some of these of mine, if long enough upheld to a clear and kindly light, may be found worthy to be cut and polished, and sometimes perchance even to be set over some fair breast. And so forth: you may roll my quaint fancy about into as many shapes as you please —unless perchance you think that already it has been rounded and worn away to your heart's content. However, "What's in a name?" Whatever you may think of my title, be assured this pouch of shingle was by me well intended. If any reader be otherwise minded, let him take my good intentions and pave his own path with them!

A word as to the fragments of reflection which

I have thrown into cadence. I do not know that a thought need lose its reflective power if expressed in verse. It ought to gain. Moreover, one use of verse is this : that in one or other of its forms we may find a channel of transpiration for some of those fancies, feelings, and thoughts, which could not otherwise be said at all, but which, if only they be well said—and "there's the rub"—it may be well for us to say. The intermingling of verse with prose may seem less unnatural now that so much of our prose is becoming rhythmical—and, shall I add, so much of our verse becoming prosy.

But I suppose I mainly threw in these variations of cadence in order to break the sameness and lighten the σεμνότης inseparable from any series of aphorisms. That necessary manner of sententiousness, and the dropping fire of that antithesis which is of the essence of Aphorism, are apt to irritate the ordinary reader by the very rattle of their mitraille. So I sought to appease this possible annoyance of cartridge by blowing now and then a bugle of rhyme. Craving indulgence for carrying on my conceit, I have, in remembrance of Wordsworth's boy, called these cadences my "shells"; and if my readers (not on that account necessarily idiotic) apply the convolutions to their ear, they also may possibly hear "murmurings from within," expressive sometimes of a "communion with their native sea."

Or else you may call them "seaweeds," if you will, spread out for you on the paper by way of change. For their intended effect is that expressed so prettily by Ausonius :

" Detegit admixtos non concolor herba lapillos."

and again :

" lucetque latetque
Calculus, et viridem distinguit glarea muscum."

Thus much for my shells, or weeds, of rhyme among my pebbles, I hope, of reason :—not but what I trust there may be found also some reason in my rhymes.

For my marginal references, I gave them because my printer had chosen for me the antique form, and it seemed ἄτοπόν τι to have a margin and nothing in it. And I was the less indisposed thereto, for it gave me scope for playing with an old love of "*la haute science de bons morceaux.*" Moreover, I excused myself the more readily in this, because I thought that if any like-minded reader should take up my book, he would thus at any rate find himself repaid by being refreshed with the memory of some of his sweet familiar melodies, and with bits of incontestable beauty and admitted wisdom. Though I have impaired my own " pebbles " by contrast, I have, at least in one sense, enriched my " pocket " to any who cares to pick it :—and so far am I from objecting to have my pocket picked, that nothing, I confess, would please me better !

I would beg my readers of their grace to remember that what to their cultured mind may seem truistic or common-place, or too long admitted to be questioned, may not all prove so to some for whose pleasure and profit I have put the better part of these thoughts together. If any of the things I have said be indeed untrue, show me their untruth and I will make ducks and drakes of them along the face of the deep. Yet if they be true, I pray you let them pass. Truths have a happy tendency to grow truistic, and such propositions, except indeed they be " identical," are not necessarily obnoxious to the charge of vacuity.

In sorting over my rough fragments, in order to send forth these as fit as in me lay, I have myself found, on holding them up to my best light, so many flaws great and small, that I shall indeed count it strange if readers of practised acumen do not find many more. If the facets of any of these pebbles be found faulty, give me a chance of another setting, and I will cut them better ! Acquit at any rate of the *cacoethes scribendi* one who hastens to close his eleventh lustrum without having gone out of the way of his primary work to make or to mar his mortal immortality ; and " what's amiss, may it be heard gently." " Facessat livor, fruatur candor."

Lastly, let me say a word as to the matters of main moment in this book—matters, I mean, expressive of the spiritual life. In these " may the wise be on my side "—yet I hold no man to be wise in this department of knowledge, who has not the insight to perceive the traits of the New Life, and who does not receive the testimony of the NEW MAN. To Him I say, with another Eastern poet, " Oh that Thy grace would cleanse my brain." Of Him we have, of course, in common with most of His people who love to reflect, many things in our mind which need not be said in any book, much less in this : but in most of the spiritual things in this book, and herein especially of the duty of the State towards JESUS, I know that I speak the truth. If any man says he sees the truth to lie in another way, why then we must have it out in the saw-pit, and to our own Master we stand or fall. I hold it wrong for Sovereign Authority not to set forth to the people the Son of Mary and of God. Such, indeed, is the face of Jesus Christ that, like the disciples on the Mount, we fail rightly to see Him though He is before us, and the Mystery of History is even more dim than that of Prophecy. But this is rather a reason for following on to know Him than for setting Him aside as one whom we will not know. If there were those who felt it their duty to hand on Confucius, it is certainly the duty of a Christian State, so far as in us lies, to hand on THE CHRIST. Plant His words in the hearts of the little ones, and give the People of the Future the chance of understanding Him better than you do. Else you leave the fortunes of the race of Englishmen, which means no small part of the race of man, to "wild hearts and feeble wings"; and you deliver the tasks of might to a sectarian weakness, which it is the duty of the Sovereign State rather to protect from all the sophisters that would lime it—yea, even from those good but short-sighted empirics, whose precious nostrums would break our head. How this can be constitutionally done remains to be seen. But, as we should expect at this time of the World's day, and of England's day, the difficulty, however complicated by our neglect, is not yet past solution.

Sed hæc hactenus. φωνᾶντα συνετοῖσιν.

South Bersted Vicarage, Bognor,
    Anno DOMINI MDCCCLXXVII.

Contents.

Contents.

Contents.

Contents.

Contents.

Contents.

Contents.

Contents.

Contents.

Contents.

Contents.

Contents.

Contents.

Contents.

Contents.

Contents.

Writer's Errata.

Page	line	for	read
11	8	with	in.
25	13	both	all.
34	2	himself	him*self.*
97	6 in margin	E	*è*
103	24, erase last eight words.		

A pocket of pebbles.

1.

LOVE, and let love.

2.

A LARGE part of life is, or ought to be, spent in making up our imperfections and redeeming old mistakes. In many a drawing, some wrong form in an early stage, some strong or misplaced light, or some unjust shadow, requires for its expunging, or its retiring, for its bringing up, or else for its keeping, valuable hours which might have been spent in doing many things in the picture which therefore have yet to be done.

Diu, res si qua diu mortalibus ulla est. *Verg.*

3.

I THINK it would give originality to style, and versatility to the modes of turning

Exemplaria versate. *Hor.*

thought, if we were to do with young Englishmen in their own language, as we do with them in Latin and Greek. As we set them to write in the style, now of Livy, Cicero, or Tacitus, now of Virgil, Lucretius, or Horace, now of Sophocles or Demosthenes, why should we not give them the advantage of practising the style, now of Johnson or of Bacon (save in archaism), now of Macaulay, or of Hooker, now of Shakespeare, and of any writer of prose or poetry who shall be regarded as exemplary?

4.

Whatsoever thy hand,&c. Eccles.

BE not lightly turned off from doing one thing to doing another. If you have made your plan to do one thing, let that, except for cogent reasons, be well done first. Do not, in an idle, vagabond way, turn off to whatever else may offer itself, for the mere pleasure of the moment. Let not your actions be swayed hither and thither by the vague currents of the hour, like those long river-weeds, to use the poet's image, which follow every movement of the waters.

At the same time I suppose it must always be a trying and painful thing for men of genius to postpone an *afflatus*; and yet the mere needs of life demand this, even when a man has no other main work; for he still has to eat, drink, and sleep, and maintain some few relations with society. How many great works do we owe to the strong sacrifice of other claims; and even the lives of very plain-going persons require a certain amount of generalship in this matter—that is, if they are wont to become really interested in any works at all.

Angustum formica terens iter.
Verg.

5.

WE may judge what a beautiful people the Greeks must have been from Aristotle's saying that to be without personal beauty must cast a shadow over the happiness of man. According to this what a wretched lot most of us must be !

6.

THESE few weeks have swept over the world like the Simoom ; they have left the world covered with fragments of crowns

Bellum, concordia, cetera, Quorum advertu manet incolumis natura abituque.
Lucr.

and shreds of thrones : and now all begins to smile again. Only the bereaved, and those who feel with them, mourn ; the map is altered ; and recreation is begun. "Thou turnest man to destruction ; again Thou sayest, Come again, ye children of men."

7.

οὐχ ἧττον ἀνθρώπ- ινα τὰ ἄλογα πάθη. *Arist.*

IN vanquishing desire, our wisdom is, not so much to bring ourselves to imagine that a wrong pleasure is not a pleasure, but, re-cognising that it *is* a pleasure of a lower kind, we must simply remember as a settled fact that pleasures which break the predica-ments of duty are wrong and therefore moreover full of danger.

8.

WHAT am I to say to a man who brings three combs round, for which he asks an exorbitant price, obviously only to walk and beg ? When a man in a parish is thrown out of work, he must either apply to the Union, or break the vagrancy law. It seems to me, that if men who are thus with-out fair means of life were always to apply to the Union, it would soon set the guardians upon organising a scheme for finding employment. Guardians would deem it wrong either to let men starve, or to sell them up and so make them a permanent burden upon the ratepayers, by reason of a temporary distress. I venture to think that there ought to be some Central Committee for receiving applications from workmen, and for ascertaining by certificate through post and telegraph the capacity and industry of these: and that then these should be directed or forwarded, by aid of funds from public or charitable sources, to be in part repaid, to places which shall have been registered as wanting hands. If I am a combmaker out of work, I ought to be able to ascertain at once who is the most convenient Combmaker that wants such a man as I am. In the event of any branch of trade being overstocked, suitable public works should employ the labour thus let loose and turned adrift. In this matter local Charity Organisation ought to be upon an understanding with the Board of Guardians and also with the State. The system of relief, either

εἷς δ' ἀνὴρ
οὐ πάνθ'
ὁρᾷ.

Eur.

outside the Union or in the casual ward, must not be too hastily modified till some such plan is arranged. But this can only be lightly touched on here.

9.

ἄλα δῖαν.
Hom.

THE voice and manner of ———— are like the voice and manner of the sea, both in the exercise and in the control of its magnificence. As, when the sea "talks" against the shore with quiet, varied music, and subdued roll, you know there is an infinite power behind it, so you feel that the free undulations of his persuasive periods speak a soul charged with multitudinous argument, to be hurled at will against any that shall oppose the course of his Cause.

10.

Desidiæ
cordi.
Verg.

μέγα
νήπιος.
Hom.

TO-DAY I said to a young student who was at home for the Cambridge Vacation, "How does the work get on?" He said in an off-hand, self-satisfied manner, "Oh! I *don't* work." I had been a Tutor; and my countenance naturally fell, and my blood was up. But the father and mother, who stood by, (I speak without exaggeration) positively laughed! Nay, but they *did* laugh. Against all the efforts of Tutors, their advice and reproof, their attempts to warn him of idleness and to induce him to learn what his father, after hard work, was paying for him to be taught, behold the approving smile of that very sire, showing himself to his son as one who regards idleness as a condition to be amused at, if not an ideal to be aimed at! How woefully the difficulties of education are enhanced by the folly of homes.

Genus in-
tractabile.
Verg.

II.

ONE of the happiest marriages I know was on this wise. A well-to-do farmer's wife died, and left a large, but small family. He had an excellent house-keeper. He became attached to her; but his love cooled, and he was for breaking it off. Nothing of the sort! Her ladyship had insight enough to see that he was only a weak man; and she knew no less well that she was a strong woman, suitable for him, and capable of doing, and wanting to do, the

Sic visum
Veneri.
Hor.

ἔργα
γυναικῶν.
Hom.

best for him ; and so she sued him there and then—" sued " for his hand. He, finding it so, like a sensible man, made the best of—I will not say a *bad* job ; for I affirm that this is one of the brightest and happiest couples I know. She never " has any words " with the first family, who respect and love her from oldest to youngest, and from first, as I hope, to last.

[This expression "has any words" suggests interesting comment, by the way, for any reader who cares to dwell on it.]

12.

THE expression, "*higher* Education," is just, for it leaves the superlative degree for that Education with which the Sovereign State seems, alas ! likely to be obliged by a conflict of morbid and unenlightened consciences to renounce its connection. Its *interest* therein it cannot renounce. Indeed the Sovereign State will find its interest in the Highest Education to be so direct, that it will be forced, in a mode which I propose to indicate elsewhere, to maintain its connection with it. When the

Their eyes were holden that they should not know Him, and He vanished out of their sight. *S. Luke.*

national conscience in its late-found freedom has played its fill with the State line, it will find itself landed again on the bank of Christianity. For Christ's is the Highest Nature, and Christian Education is the highest culture; and this the Sovereign State will find that it cannot afford to leave to Church Tom, Nonconformist Dick, or Atheist Harry.

13.

HOW soon passing events become the subject of painting, poetry, and history. We move and act among them, and are a part of them to-day. To-morrow, like Aeneas, who saw his own doings on the brazen gates of the Tyrian Queen, we have the whole hung in galleries or described in books, and moving us again, sometimes to indignation, sometimes to tears.

14.

SOME always think that everything is against them. In moods of discontent or unhappiness it is astonishing what trifles can assume an air of antagonism.

Is not my word a hammer that breaketh the rock in pieces? Jer. xxiii. 29

A PARSON'S business is that of a stone-breaker. But there is usually not a stone-breaker in the parish who has such hard work before him. The power of converting people ought, it seems to me, to be a primary requisite in the eyes of those who pass Christian ministers into Holy Orders.

15.

YE lovers, be not one-eyed. If, oh eligible young woman, a man has home and land and money, but not love, you will *of course* not be such a little fool as to wish for him because of those? But if he profess love for you before he has a home and fair means of common life to offer you, or at least a good hope of these within reasonable time, his love, whatever it may turn to afterwards, is now but an airy, ideal, theoretical, unembodied, unsubstantial thing, not yet the least to be leaned on. Love, if we would personify the little god completely, must have both substance and spirit —a fair amount of wit being taken for granted.

" Poco di matto."

16.

THE sailor pulls his boat to the land, not the land to his boat. Woe to the man who tries to shift what is in its nature abiding: his object rather should be to land himself thereon.

17.

SEEING that no right-minded man liveth to himself alone, it might seem uninteresting, not to say stupid—except we have to get our bread by it—to steep ourselves with any special knowledge which none shall have but we. This however is sometimes made up for and rendered rational, if men leave behind them books which keep for the use of the rising, changing, and growing world the upshot of the exercise of special gifts. Such may become useful some day, except their chosen topics be in their very nature useless. I am told of a man who had, I suppose, been rummaging about in a great Library, and who fell asleep and dreamt the following ghastly line: " Immemorabilium per furva crepuscula palpans," which his learned brother translates, " Fumbling among the tawny twilights of things un-rememberable."

18.

THE effect of living near so changeful an element as the sea makes up to the mind in some sort for the absence of human con-verse. Not but what the old classical sculptors always made their sea-gods melancholy.

19.

IF you find a man putting himself unduly forward, you will often discover that it is because his circumstances have put him unduly backward. He, knowing himself better, naturally selects himself as fit to survive. Have mercy on a man who naturally selects himself the more, when nobody else selects him! Self-preservation is a law, if not the first law, even of the Christian life. ' Extravagance of all sorts is often to be explained by this. Some people would rather be infamous than not famous ; or known by some eccentricity rather than not known at all. If any of my

readers has enjoyed the rare luck of having
been let alone to indulge his own real or un-
real genius, *appone lucro.* "*Nec vixit male qui
natus moriensque fefellit*" may have a great
deal of truth in it if a man knows himself, and
knows his God, and loves his neighbour as
himself. But the State is, I suppose,
coming to learn the importance, if only
for its own peace and quietness, of appor-
tioning to each, especially to the active and
irritable, their suitable spheres. The insolence of men out of office, as administrators well know, is quelled and quashed
by investing them with the responsibility
of office. If men are not put in the way of
living their own proper lives, they will become eternal disturbers of other people's
lives.

οὐκ οἶδ'·
ἃ γὰρ
δρῶσ' οἱ
κρατοῦν-
τες οὐχ
ὁρῶ.
    Soph.

Plausumque
pennis Dat
tecto
ingentem,
mox aere
lapsa quieto
Radit iter
liquidum
celeres neque
commovet
alas.
    Verg.

20.

THOSE who live always in natural and
rightful enjoyment must perforce fail to
realize the keenness of relish with which a
man always steeped in unnatural misery
welcomes such an enjoyment, as from time
to time it comes.

21.

σποδοῦ
λέβητας
εὐθέτους.
Æsch.

CREMATION of the dead would be only like burning of the weeds, instead of letting them decay.

22.

Furum
aviumque
maxima
formido.
Verg.

THE man who keeps pounding on with effete denunciations against evils and dangers long gone by, is like that mawkin, which at first indeed took his place in the seed-time of a wheat-field, and so was highly useful ; but which remains hanging out ghastly arms and mimic rags, even after the summer is ended, the harvest past, and the wheat gathered into the garner—a comic anachronism amid the stubble and the pigs.

Insidias
avium
moliri.
Verg.

Let him put himself by, and hang out again when dangers again rise, and the like evils call for him—which they are sure enough to do in the round of Time ; for evil, like history, of which it forms the main part, repeats itself.

23.

THE poles of their natures are to some persons Beauty and Duty.

24.

IT is curious to observe, how much more enormous and outrageous we are apt to count a piece of dishonesty, if we ourselves are pinched by it. The other day a man in my neighbourhood was dishonest about an Insurance business. I thought it sad, and a heinous thing in the land;—but only when I found afterwards that this very man had actually taken a tax out of my own pocket and not paid it into the Bank—my indignation knew no bounds. *Tum demum* I felt what a crime dishonesty was !

Nunc altè volnus adactum. Verg.

25.

THE world is fouler than some, and cleaner than others can imagine.

26.

THE upheaping sands of centuries cover the sunken wrecks of Churches and States, so that you can see only the outlines of their skeletons, the top of the bow, and the top of the ribs, and perhaps the jagged top of a broken mast; sharp and dangerous, when the water is mid-way between high tide and

Trudunt res ante ruuntque impetibus crebris. Lucr.

low, to any unhappy boat which the waves may drop on them. These wrecks of old vessels on new sands are like nothing so much as the fragmentary remains of old empires upon modern lands, either in the form of the frame-work of laws, or the remnants of amphitheatres, or in the names of places, and imperishable customs.

27.

IT would be interesting to work out in what ways Bible-studying people have by that agency become *quasi*-Semitic.

What advantage hath the Jew ? Much every way. *St. Paul.*

28.

EXCEPT a man's Will have perfect control over his time, it is a good thing sometimes to enter under an amicable obligation to spend it in his chosen occupation under circumstances which, however otherwise inconvenient, may foster work. This gives an intellectual as well as a moral *rationale* for at least temporary conventual life or "retreats." I wonder that bachelors who love study, and can afford it, do not oftener arrange to live together.

It is not good that the man should be alone.

29.

I HAVE known Chairmen, in their excessive pursuance of fairness and indifference, overvault themselves and fall on the other side, and positively throw ridiculous advantages into the hands of persons of known factiousness, and pronounced hostility to fairness : whereby they truly show themselves " indifferent " Chairmen.

τίς ὧδε
τέκνοισι
Ζῆν᾽ ἄ-
βουλον
εἶδεν ;
Soph.

30.

WHEN you give anything away, as money, you should not do so with a feeling of triumph in the power of disposal, but with humility, and with a sense of responsibility to the Giver of all things good.　We have nothing which we have not received.　This, like most of these things, is not new.　Enough if I remind my readers and myself that it is *true.*

As good
stewards of
the manifold
grace of God
S. Peter.

31.

To let an opportunity go is the act of a fool ; but in the polarity of stupidity, to go out of your way for disaster and to go to market for sorrow is the act of a madman.

καιρὸς
βραχὺ
μέτρον
ἔχει.
Pind.

32.

Rev. xxii. 4.

IT is well in the case of the Church and the Scriptures that the superstitious fears of the world have guarded and kept them unmeddled with till the time came for this great work to be done well by a generation which has men who are not only good, but instructed unto the kingdom of heaven. What a satisfaction it is, for instance, to borrow a small illustration, that the embankments of the Thames, and the renewal of London were not carried out more completely in an age which did not understand the principles of engineering. How much there would have been to be undone and done again. One of the most interesting Churches in Sussex has been by its restoration rendered incapable of being restored. The letter-worship of the Jews saved the letter, and thus the spirit, of the Old Testament. The despotism of Rome saved the framework of the mediæval Church, as the mud of Tiber has saved many a fair marble form.

We lit upon her laid in Tiber ooze,
Discountenanced with centuries of slime;
All form and feature seemed, alas! to lose
What trace she once had known of touch sublime:
What thrifty man but straightway might refuse,
Counting it reckless waste of golden time,
So cheap and cumbersome a thing to choose
For aught but binding highways with her lime?
But we were idle; so we laved her face,
And whitened limb by limb with growing care—
When lo! a resurrection of rare grace!
What majesty divine! what queenly air!
And now she stands aloft in honoured place,
And men repeat her beauty everywhere.

33.

RATIONAL wonder is but the opening of the mind to draw the breasts of knowledge.

34.

THE laws of nature must be qualified by the laws of society. The man who forgets this runs his head at every turn against living walls harder than a block.

35.

THE power of speaking ought obviously to be commensurate with the power of writing; for the same mental power, be it great or small, is at the bottom of both. This inequality is a question of *pace*, and is a superable accident. If indeed in his writing a man do not accustom himself to have his thoughts in fair order before he so expresses himself, then it is only to be expected that his tongue will hang fire just as his pen does, and his failure in eloquence may be fairly set down as his own fault. But many men who write *currente calamo* cannot speak on the very same topic with running tongue. How is this? It is be-

cause the pace at which he writes must at
its quickest be slower than the pace requisite for a fluent oration. To remove this
incongruity, the symbols of written language
must be so arranged as to admit of the
same pace in writing as in speaking. Then
he who can write with facility will naturally
and from uniform pace of thought be able
also to speak with facility.

36.

A MAN with leisure and education is like
one on horseback in a lane in the blackberry
season. He can get fine, ripe blackberries,
that have been beyond the reach of the little
vulgar boy. Who does not envy such high
riders ?

37.

PEOPLE sometimes do dispassionately
and after long deliberation, earnest con-
sideration, and reconsideration, things more
wild and outrageous than other people do by
the first impulse of their common sense.
This is true sometimes of the very same
persons !

38.

MEN of place and in the position of administrators should encourage able men of good memory to attach themselves to able men of clever talk and power of rapid conclusion, so that the value of none be lost. Care ought to be taken in all regions of the State to supplement power with power. Let a detailed education provide the right men, and then let wise administration put all in the right place. Power of speaking, and power of writing, which seldom co-exist, should be noted and provided for. Competitive examination has not yet fully looked this in the face.

39.

EVERYBODY claims to be moderate. I have never heard more intemperate speeches than in the advocacy of Temperance!

40.

IN the solemn management of our life, we may have and maintain our larger works, and our fixed and life-long aims. These must not be wholly dropped because of our professional or our smaller daily and occasional duties, even though these latter should oblige a man to hold the former for a more or less long time in abeyance, or to do them not nearly so well as he might if he could be *totus in illis*. What to do and what not to do, what pertains and what does not pertain to our eternal life, what is a primary and what a secondary duty, and what is not a duty at all, but merely a useless and illegitimate pleasure, is often a painful question. "Gather up the fragments, that nothing be lost" refers closely to *time* in this regard.

οὐδὲν πρὸς Διόνυσον.

41.

IN public speaking, or in treating of any subject, be original amidst your accurate array of facts, and have a bony framework of knowledge underlying the nerves of your originality ; else what you say is flaccid and pulpy stuff, and not lively oracle.

42.

IF any of our emotions of love or our impulses of affection begin from our spirit

Witless pity breedeth fruitless love.
Fairfax.

and flow to the spirit of the object, then and then only are they in order. It is from the bottom of the soul that love should take its rise. To be moved towards another in other wise than from the heart is out of place, and is disturbing and dangerous. We cannot desire more than one at a time from the heart; and if such a desire be held in due check by social obligation, a man cannot, I should think, go far wrong in these matters. It is, however, only the Spirit proceeding from the Father and the Son Who can order all emotions duly.

"Love one, and love no more."

Nec liquidi corrumpitur usus olivi. *Verg.*

43.

IT is wise to dwell, not on physical possibilities, but on moral impossibilities.

44.

THERE are a good many things to be said as to the hopeful prospects of temperance, and among them this:—that the removal of intemperance from the lower classes is a more likely event than was that partial removal of it which has already

taken place with the upper classes. There
are reasons why it should be removable from
those, which did not tend or help to remove
it from these—from whom it has nevertheless
been removed. These had leisure which
did not demand its abatement, and yet
it abated. They were not quickened in
breaking it off by the lack of means to
keep it on; yet they broke it off. There
was no fear of destitution staring them in
the face. There was no pressure from
starving wives and clamorous families.
The lower classes have both these incen-
tives. Moreover, education was not brought
to bear in the same systematic way upon
the upper classes, who, far from being
regularly educated, were scantly, as a rule,
morally trained. This great engine is
being brought to bear on the lower classes,
and will in each year have higher and
wider play. The children of the people
are being taught in orderly fashion to
spend time well, to energise faculties into
facilities, and to learn the value of money
—how to get it, use it, and save it. Besides,
teachers and ministers had little to do with

Nocturnique
orgia Bacchi
Verg.

καρδίας
δηκτήρια.
Eur.

minishing this vice in the upper classes; among the lower they are constantly bringing to bear praise and blame, and are creating a sense of shame, to which the lower classes are at least equally open. Lastly, the former abatement was not due to any organised efforts of Temperance Societies, which are doing so much among the people. From these reasons there is a greater chance that drunkenness will be mitigated among the "lower" classes also.

45.

IF you lightly take gifts, you bind yourself and you blind yourself.

46.

NOT only in word, but too often in mood also, there is but an iota of difference between the æsthetic and the atheistic.

47.

TAKE care not to give way too far to that feeling of universal sympathy, whose frequent formula is, "it is all the same." It soon comes to universal apathy.

48.

WHO has not noticed that some of the most crucial, telling, obstinate, and deter-mined observations are often made with a yawn, as the heart of a letter is sometimes deferred to the postscript? Always take the more careful note of what a man says to you with a yawn!

Ἄπολλον Ἀποτρό-παιε, τοῦ χασμή-ματος.
Aristoph.

49.

IN the march of mind it is habitual for writers to beat down their predecessors, and to tread ruthlessly over their carcases the moment they have fallen. It may well be so where the impressions of such writers have been based on facts wholly false, but it is too much our habit to forget that, when facts have all been before the mind, the special impressions of men are all valuable so far as they are genuine, no matter who comes before or after other.

50.

THE discovery of truth is often, but most unjustly, retarded by the laugh raised at some isolated failure of an early enquirer.

For instance, when the fossil salamander of Oiningen quarries, which Scheuchzer styled in 1726 *homo diluvii testis*, was shown by Peter Campa in 1787 to be a reptile.

51.

Ye know not what manner of spirit ye are of.
CHRIST.

OUR own moods vary widely, yet we cannot at the moment precisely comprehend our being in a mood entirely different from the one in which we are.

52.

A. B. and C., that is, the world at large, value the spirit of independence and proper pride in D. Why? Because D is the less likely to pester them for money. A. B. and C. are not wholly wrong ; but do not let it be supposed that their admiration is wholly moral and ingenuous.

53.

PRAYERS which are inaudible, are naturally best adapted for the hearing of the Invisible : yet the air being also His, it is natural that this also should vibrate with the voice of prayer.

Some fowl is warbling for my joy—but where
I weet not : wistfully I gaze
Through all the tremulous round of leafage there ;
Bending and leaning slantwise, lo ! I raise
Peering enquiry for my fount of praise—
That half-articulate sonneteer, too rare
To be commended in elaboured lays :—
Ah me ! I fail to find her anywhere—
Blest could I know who blesses me.   'Tis so
I prove the sweet effects of some kind soul,
Whose wishes waft about me as I go;
I feel some hidden help doth make me whole.
How like that sightless song this soundless
    prayer !
Some one is praying for me :—tell me, where ?

πυκνό-
πτεροι δ'
εἴσω κατ'
αὐτὸν
εὐστομ-
οῦσ' ἀηδό-
νες.
Soph.

54.

CASUISTRY is a long name and a hard word ; and its field is one in which, without guidance from above, simple minds may lose themselves. For instance, pride, we know, comes before destruction ; but is it always easy to separate pride from that sense of manhood and joy of courage, which is part of the very essence of true nobility ? Without remembering thankfully that it comes from God, and that in Him we live and move and have our strength, this very spirit of manhood drivels down into the isolation of devilry.

Again, is it always very easy to say at what point just indignation becomes sinful anger, and where we do well to be angry, and where we do ill ? If we allow ourselves to be so indignant as to take the law into our own hands, we forget that we are not as God. Yet if we contemplate wrong with equanimity, and make no move to avert it, we leave undone our part as men. Here again, except we fall back on the infinite and Almighty Governour, we do or suffer sad disaster. There is a time to speak and a

ɔur peace. Sometimes, though
y be hot within us, we must
uth as it were with a bridle,
ɡodly act and talk in our sight

re is the border-land between
tion and inordinate. An emo-
ʋe the very colour of heaven,
turned black by the slightest
ɔme practical forgetfulness of
ɩ shalt not."
difficulties which must occur
ɩs, and nothing but trust in
ɪide can help us. There is
d round all morals, and the
ɾest attaches to well-written
    Christian novelists and
ramatists, when such arise
pure genius and matured by
ɩich can be properly termed
have before them a field of
What "houses" will be drawn
na of the New Man! What
ow in the boxes of Mudie or
Smith when some of the best
w give us are gone out. It

Agnosco
veteris ves-
tigia flammæ
Virg.

τὸ γὰρ
δίκαιον
οἶδε καὶ
τραγῳδία.

marks a signal advance in Literature when the Christian Poet steps on the Stage, and in Religion when a Bishop allows us to listen to him.

55.

TAKE care of the proverb : "Wherever there's smoke there's fire :"—that smoke very often arises from that little member which is set on fire of hell.

ἐμβαλὼν
σπινθῆρα
μικρόν.
Aristoph.

56.

SOME people whip the simple mental operations, which must necessarily take place in all but idiotic brains, into a spume and flummery of verbiage, full of air bubbles and occupying more space than the world has room or time for. But I forgot I was myself putting together a book : *caveat emptor !*

σήματα
λυγρά.
Hom.

57.

" LORD, teach us to pray" did not merely mean "give us words to say" but "teach us what it is, in the heat of the day, among the trees of this regained garden, to walk and to talk with our Father."

58.

HOW are you to meet, accost, address, and benefit a parishioner, your knowledge of whose inner difficulties and whose language in your parish compels you to speak to him, but who, perhaps with reason, has set down your intellect as incapable of instructing him. You must use no single touch of irony, or you will make him hate both you and your Master ; but triumph over his pride by manifesting the reality of your regard for him. " Is there no light which you can get from me upon any of your knotty points ? I will task myself to study for you any such point, if not familiar with the question." If obliged to use indignant language as to his influence on others, take care that he shall not be able to regard it as personal from yourself. If you can speak with a touch of sad good-humour, so much the better ; and if without offence you can pleasantly give him reason to alter his view of your capacity and your knowledge, better still. But if you can persuade him to come and see JESUS, that is best of all. Thou hast " gained thy brother."

Mollissima fandi Tempora, quis rebus dexter modus. Verg.

59.

Let your
light, &c.
Christ.

A POET, to be a dramatist, should forget himself; but in other moods he should generally remember himself, and so each way be useful to his generation and to the ongoing world. He should merge himself in ideal situations, because we want to know what men in general are; but his thoughts should breathe their own aroma, and his words burn with their own fire, because we want to know what the best men in particular are.

60.

IN matters of marked import, most successful lines of vigorous action, at least in gentle minds, are a mean between diffidence and dash.

61.

Jesus Himself stood in the midst of them.
St. Luke.

BE very careful to accommodate your modes of thought and your views of personal ambition, not to what this or that person thinks high and low, but to what *is* high and low, true and false, and the like. "Nearer my God to Thee" must be our motto.

62.

HOW are we to regard that which we have not, but which we think it would be good for us to have? All such things from lowest to highest come under the same rule. That rule is quite clear. We must not fasten our minds on anything, except habits of excellence, and say, "I mean to attain that, come what may." It is unrestful, and in some degree dangerous—I do not say it is irreligious, but *dangerous*—even with respect to a lawful object of ambition, to fix our gaze on it and go through *fas* to get it, for the temptation may be sore to go through *nefas* also. Not but what a man may be so penetrated with a sense of his powers that he may be convinced, and in some sort may feel inspired with the conviction, that to work them in some unattained sphere may be his duty— ἔργον δυνάμει μετρεῖται. But to live rightly under this conviction, and to rest faithfully amidst these endeavours, requires constant watchfulness. A man must be very careful not to form any fixed idea that God wants him for any special work. If the work is mani-

His amor unus erat, pariterque in bella ruebant. *Verg.*

Rerum pars altera adempta est. *Verg.*

Moriens animam abstulit hosti. *Verg.*

festly to be done and nobody else can do it, especially if it be near at hand, and the time for its doing be passing or about to pass, then in God's name let him 'go gallantly on,' as the great Chevalier, Arnold's friend, told me he had said to Florence Nightingale ; but even then let him be humbly prepared at any moment to find the cup of his purpose suddenly put aside from his lips. Many, as the man I last named, have come to the edge of their hopes of great work, and had but a peep into the land where other men were to enter into their labours. But these high examples go beyond my original purpose. I began to write this rather that by help of God I might clear and establish what has to be said about the hopes and desires of common life. Suppose I see before me or beside me, but not within my reasonable reach, a condition which commends itself to my imagination as highly adapted to my powers and my tastes. The fact that this *seems* so is to be entirely merged, drowned, and lost in the fact that it is not within my reach. Circumstances stand round me and

sever me from that object of my wishes.
God makes them stand there. What *seems*
is imagination, however vivid it may be.
All that lies in the land of uncertainty. It
may be a ghost. It may be a picture painted
by the devil. Indeed, being clean contrary
to what God allows to me, it is most probable, nay I may say certain, that it is one
of the *fata Morgana*, one of the mephitic
ignes fatui, called up by the foul fiend in
the bad airs of selfishness; an image, or
child of desire, which has nothing to do
with my Father and my God, except to
flout and oppose His omniscient love for
me. To hanker after it were vanity; to
follow it, insanity.

63.

" I LAY down my life for the sheep":—as
though Christ had said, " I take the course.
which brings the world back to God. I
cannot establish my Kingdom in the world
as it is, and live. I offer myself to God,
come life, or come, as I know it must, death.
I must go through this society of the now
men. This means death. I incur it. I show

τά γ' ἔργα
μου πε-
πονθότ'
ἐστί.

Soph.

my people this path to Heaven by my obedience unto death. God accepts me thus, together with all those who take my example, or who are ready to take it, if called to do so, even to death. This is my mode of Atonement, of setting man at one with God. This is how I lift Man. If I declined death, I should show you a wrong way, and should not bring sinners back to God. I accept death, and thus offer myself and them as a sacrifice to God, and so I reconcile you to God, though it costs my blood. In me God regards you as his perfectly reconciled children. Sacrifice and offering in the heathen way Thou wouldest not, neither hadst pleasure therein. Then said I, Lo I come—in the Volume of the Book it is written of me—*to do Thy will*, oh God : yea, I delight to do it, Thy Law is within my heart." This is how Christ redeems us with His blood, and this contains all the idea of " substitution " which a holy soul will ask, or which the moral and spiritual sense can grasp.

64.

ONE of the most fearful ways by which you can deteriorate, is by thinking other people bad, especially the other sex. If you hold an idea that they are mostly given to sin and careless of character, as some love to maintain, your soul is apt to come crashing down like a house with dry-rot; or like the lungs of a man long diseased, that slough off into cavernous death.

Fandi fictor.
 Verg.

ὡς
πτεροῤ-
ῥυεῖ.
Aristoph.

65.

THOSE whom love couples love will hold so fast,
That love at first will still be love at last.

66.

THE worst of your becoming worse is when you do not know it. But if you light upon some old friend, or find some old piece of your writing, it is very melancholy to be smitten with the sense—"*quantum mutatus ab illo.*" Yet you may bethink you for your comfort that in other ways you may be changing for the better. What, however, is the set of the main current of your being?

παλιμ-
μήκη
χρόνον
τιθεῖσαι
τρίβῳ.
Æsch.

67.

SHIP TO TUG.

STRUGGLING with score of sails I barely strain
In painful progress o'er this windless deep;
I count me happy if across the main
Some straggling breeze shall come and kindly
     keep
My heavy sides from sinking into sleep :—
What is it speeds thee o'er the watery plain,
Thou mimic craft, and lends thee life to leap
And leave me, laughing at my voyage vain ?
I see there is a something in thy heart
Which gives a force to thee I may not know;
To me, I pray, that secret power impart,
That I may learn some surer way to go,
Nor trust the lazy winds that puff and lull,
And leave me in the lurch, a lumbering hull.

68.

TUG TO SHIP.

Poor barque, it grieves me sore to see thee lie
So idly murmuring on that breathless bed;
Come, without more ado, and deftly tie
This good stout hawser 'neath thy figure-head;
Life in my inmost heart I have, so I
Though the wind breathe not, never feel as
    dead.
Come, let me draw thee with me; by and by
To thy fair haven thou shalt thus be sped:
Thou art, I see, like those sad sons of men
That trust to make their way, nor look for
    grace;
They start with all their goodly freight, and
    then,
When winds of feeling fail, they lose the race;
But bind thyself to me, and thy desire
Shall pluck the mystery of my heart-fed fire.

νήνεμος
αἰθρῃ.
Hom.

69.

WHICH begins first, faith or knowledge? Who can say? With children probably faith; but to a man who has grown up in ignorance of God, the observation of some fact, or else the attaining some piece of knowledge about Him is accompanied by belief in the way of simultaneity. Then, believing that He is, you find reward if you diligently seek Him. To know Him is to love Him. This is to be at peace. Amidst pains and distresses of body, mind, and estate, you rest on the Eternal, notwithstanding all passing changes. Nobody truly believes it to be so, till he finds it to be so. Everybody who finds it to be so "believes." All men find it to be so whom we commonly call "good," for reverence enters into our idea of goodness. The existence of the Father can however be arrived at both by analysis and synthesis. Every examined detail leads you up to God, Whom hitherto you knew not; and taking God for the foundation and starting point of observation, knowing in Whom you believe, you descend to the details of creation and Providence by the

Placato possum non miser esse Deo.   *Ov.*

same chain by which you might, logically speaking, have climbed. Morally speaking, can the soul climb without some sort of belief? that is the question. It is akin to that enquiry as to the priority, connateness, or posteriority of matter or spirit, which probably is above demonstration. Here faith answers in the analogy to spirit; the appreciation of fact, to matter. It is true that "the honest and good heart" will reach God, either mediately or immediately; but then the honest and good heart is not wholly ignorant of God to begin with. Such a heart, like the sound syllogism, involves the *Petitio Principii*; only, instead of reaching his Universal through an enumeration of particulars, a process not here applicable, he finds Him by an examination of the one great crucial Instance Himself.

70.

THERE is here no private Secretary, except Conscience, to prevent the Majesty of Heaven from being constantly assailed by the petitions of fools.

71.

"WHAT are men better than sheep and goats, that nourish a blind life within the brain, if, knowing God, they lift not hands of prayer, both for themselves, and those that call them friend? For thus the whole round world is every way bound by gold chains about the feet of God." How much *worse* than goats are those who do not care to know anything of God, when they might know him through Jesus! And these men assume to lead an advanced civilization! Was ever science so foolishly so called? Call it "inscience" or "nescience," but not "pre-science" or "conscience," or any composite of science which is not negative. A farmer tells me that of a flock of 200 sheep the bell-wether went into a deep and narrow dike; 90 followed him and were choked in the mud, or lay "far-weltered" on the top of one another till they perished. So shall it be with part of this generation.

72.

SEEK to be happy more than affluent;
Wealth lies in coffers, comfort in content.

73.

FOR thirty pieces of silver Judas sold his Saviour to the Priests and himself to the devil. The whole spiritual world seemed nothing to him, and a little hard cash seemed everything. When it was too late, he saw it all. This was not an exceptional sin, save incidentally. It is so with all sin. Every man who prefers pleasure to duty is of the company of Judas. It is only in circumstantial detail that he is less infamous.

74.

Be feasting not thy habit, but thy treat,
And rather eat to live than live to eat.

75.

WE may fight like caged birds with social lies, but if there is the least colour given, they are too strong for us.

76.

IT may indeed not be good for a man to be alone—but it is infinitely better than being with any one with whom he ought not to be.

77.

A FRIEND of mine, who is a linguist, tells me that when he learns a new language, he begins by writing its grammar. So let the man who wishes to cultivate the spiritual life study the laws thereof for himself. He must not *simply* go upon books of devotion made by others, though upon these he may well lean, as when a person learns to skate. Indeed all the best men and women maintain their most advanced spiritual life by feeding on such diet, especially on the highest fare which is before them. What I here lay stress upon is, that the life of the spirit cannot be learned by merely paying attention to what is outside our own soul. Spiritual life is a ἕξις as well as an ἐπιστήμη, and cannot be duly appreciated as knowledge by the student who is not of a nature to receive it. This is why men merely scientific fail to see the beauty and truth of Christianity. They bring to the examination of the highest phenomena only the same kind of eye which serves them in the lower. They see nothing, and then employ the authority of their acquired eminence in "science" to persuade

Privata cibo natura animantûm diffluit.
Lucr.

They found it even so, but Him they saw not.
S. Luke.

men that there is nothing to see! As for those who look to them for guidance in matters higher than apes and acids, motes and moths, embryos and gases, we know that "if the blind lead the blind, both shall fall into the ditch"; and the sooner the better for the world—I do not say for themselves.

Nec quid-quam tibi prodest Aerias tentasse domos animoque rotundum percurrisse polum mori-turo. Hor.

78.

WHEN the Psalmist says "Shall the dead rise up and praise Thee?" in Christ's name, and in the light of His Love, we thankfully answer 'yes.' If the Psalmist, even without our experience and our additional ground of faith, found in that limited trust in his God enough to live upon, how much more ought *we* gratefully to feel that in this our Father's House, which His Son has prepared for us, we "have enough and to spare?"

All things are yours— whether.. life or death. St. Paul.

79.

THE people who want to make out that the Scripture is false, are generally, if not universally, those who know that they are on the way to be damned if it be true.

Thy wish was father to that thought. Shaks.

AN OLD SONG.

AND dost thou wonder, love, if soon
　　I shall be as I am to-day?
If passion is a passing boon
　　Which winds that bring will bear away?

Thy fears, my tender little one,
　　If true in part, are false in whole;—
For, grant that passion will be gone,
　　Hath nothing quickened in the soul?

Grant that, in Nature's ripening growth,
　　Some flowers of feeling we forget,
Hereby I plight thee, love, my troth
　　The fruit is now already set.

Love's orchard, trust me, is akin
　　To that the Western maids of old
So duly husbanded; within
　　The apples are of purest gold.

No bound of blooth my plat shall bear;
　　And every tree, one fruitage done,
Shall show, each month of every year,
　　Another, and another one.

And as we gather from the wise
　　That feelings fall as fashions grow,
While those sweet usages arise
　　Fresh feelings shall about them blow.

1852.

80.

IF, which I hardly believe, there are any sane and genuine Christians who wish to drive Christ and the Bible from the schools of the people, let me remind them that they must not regard this dismissal of Christianity as a merely negative concession. They may say they feel compelled by their conception of fairness not to force a teaching which some ratepayers may not agree with. But that is not a fair statement of the case. Their conception of fairness is itself unfair. If indeed the majority be made up of unbelievers, then godlessness carries the day and generations go to the dogs. But I do not now argue with such persons. I argue with Christian people, and wish to show them that a fair sense of fairness would not compel them, but on the other hand would compel them not, to swell the ranks of the enemy. I implore them to remember that *not to teach Christ* is a form of *teaching not-Christ*. And this is a positive form of teaching to which Christian people cannot in fairness be asked to lend themselves. *They* have a conscience. It becomes in

Tarda sit illa dies et nostro serior ævo.
Ov.

Impia te rationis inire elementa viamque Indugredi sceleris.
Lucr.

Cæsarem portas et fortunas ejus.
Cæsar.

practice a dogma as direct as any in the repertory of Rome. It uses the authority of the State to place the Master nowhere. Even supposing the children are among the few who have someone to care for their souls on the Sunday, what sharp child would not say to his chapel-teachers, " The *Queen* does not think it worth while to tell me anything about all this in the whole course of her careful training of me. Her most gracious Majesty would certainly do so if there were anything in it. She therefore teaches me that there is nothing in it : Victoria I know, and Her Board-master I know, but who are ye ?"

φθόγγον
ἀραῖον
οἴκοις.
Æsch.

81.

A MAN of no original genius, but with a certain sense of poetry and power of music, might gain no ordinary fame as a poet almost by the mere adaptation of the expressions of Shakespeare, if he were craftily to cull them and string them into necklaces of song. He would indeed have to guard τὸ λανθάνειν, seeing that critics are not altogether ignorant of poets' devices.

82.

IN religion it mostly is, as in philosophy it always was, that men get hold of a set of theories, chop them into hard phrases, boil them up with verbiage, and pour them on our devoted heads. The one extreme cry "Church, Church," when they have no Church, or only a formal one. The other commonly disports itself in dilating upon high-sounding abstractions. It seems to me that religious teaching should first seek to impart the seed of the New Life, and then tackle with the facts and puzzles of the heart and conscience, bringing the healing power to bear on these one by one. Face the special malady:—"Where does the pain lie? what is its cause?" That being discovered, rise to your special cure, your special text, your special truth—your theory, if you have got one for the occasion. Otherwise theoretic preaching too often flies in the air ὑπὲρ ἄστρων βέλος ἠλίθιον. Not but what it is wholesome to expatiate with reverent love on the high and grand graces and virtues of the absolutely divine life, and to reason well on immortality.

Quare Religio (Christiana) pedibus neglecta vicissim obteritur. *Lucr.*

Æsch.

This is true philosophy, though not to be used to the exclusion of the more special and practical teaching of which I have spoken. The other mode is not philosophy in any sense. It often works upon the bargain supposed to have been gone through by the Eternal Father and Jesus, in a manner far more nauseating, if possible, than those other modes of treating religious questions, to which some objections are partially reasonable.

Moniti meliora sequamur. *Verg.*

83.

THE great game-license of Eden " Have dominion over the beast of the field," must, *mutatis mutandis*, be exercised over godless people in the land. We do so when they themselves commit crimes, but, though in putting by the restraint of God's Presence, they propagate the principles which make other people criminals, yet Birmingham would fain set such persons in the seat of God, and model education to the limits which they demand. So completely do they turn the tables and reverse the aforesaid license, that they say "Have dominion over the

τὰ δ' ἔνθεν οὔτ' εἶδον οὔτ' ἐννέπω.   *Æsch.*

children of this Christian nation, oh 'beasts of the people.'" Ten thousand children cry to the School Board for the bread of the best life. School Board replies, "We all want you to have it, except some few of God's enemies among us who don't like to pay their penny in the pound for it : so you must all, dear children, go to the devil, as far as we can help you in the matter." Is this high statesmanship? Who does not see that an enemy does this? And it is the part of an enemy to let it be done. How plainly would the Destroyer checkmate the Saviour if he could get the Sovereign State to push the Bible from the Schools. The King indeed never can be taken, but our game is lost if He may not move.

Dabit deus his quoque finem. Verg.

τὸν πάντα δ' ὄλβον ἦμαρ ἐν μ' ἀφεί-λετο.

Eur.

84.

"A piece of work" is made by haste; but cease,
Fume not, and you will make *a work of peace*.

85.

OUR power of overcoming evil by good depends mainly on our power of compassion.

86.

THE order of our physical κόσμος, as you would expect from the Unity of God, finds a parallel in our moral life. In both, order is preserved by a combination of movements. The movement of the earth round the sun is arranged co-ordinately with its motion round its axis. The result of these combined movements is the sensation of repose. So in morals there is a general law of right under which human spirits come. But there is also a social law, and there are obligations varying with the individual, which serve as a compensative check, and so preserve society in courses fairly even, and which aim at the perfect figure. But— as says *il Maestro di color che sanno*—τὰ φύσει θειότερα.

Semotum ab rerum motu placidâque quiete.
Lucr.

87.

HOW awful it is to see a man sporting with unmannerly and unmanly recklessness on the brink of the precipice of pleasure. This is only the more plainly true because it is trite.

Pollicitus meliora.

88.

THE rising Spirit of the New Man by all laws of growth must more and more rapidly master, and more and more lightly wield inert matter to His desired modes. The stronger the Spirit shows Himself, the less massive, and the more manageable matter becomes. Matter has no innate strength. The dead weight of its influence on Spirit causes that irregularity called Evil. The person whom Christ addressed when He said, " Get thee behind Me, Satan," and "it is written," can have no direct influence upon the Divine Spirit, but seems to use the forms and circumstances of matter to create confusion. The fear is, lest the Divine Spirit, in the present stage of His working, be modified and limited by that remnant of the old Adam which degrades some of His best recipients ; and so lest new forms be worse than the old. If Freedom succeed in cutting the Church out of the Nation, the last state of parts of this land may come to be worse than Druid-worship. It is monstrous that the New Creature should, by naturally selecting its own elimination, permit the

Horum even-
ta videbis.
Lucr.

survival of the unfittest as the Sovereign Power in the State. Have those alone no conscience who feel it right to keep Christ in the State and the Bible in the Schools? If Christ is to be thrust forth from these, then nobody's conscience is considered except the conscience of those who ignore conscience! For the man who says "There is no God, so I won't pay for one," is the person who is at the bottom of all this pretended claim for a suicidal toleration. Christians would agree, at least as to Bible-teaching, were it not for the infidel. We can get over every difficulty but him. This is shown by the battle of Birmingham. The Atheist in the name of Freedom stands clapping his wings on his dung-hill. Truth has in truth made him externally too free, and this is the way the slave repays her for having gone a step too far! An overstrained toleration has put arms and fire into the hands of God's enemy; and, mastered by the modern phrase, the people affect to love to have it so, but in reality they *hate* to have it so. *Quousque, Domine?*

Stygii caput implacabile fontis.
Verg.

ἀκόλαστος ὄχλος κρείσσων πυρός.
Eur.

δίκης ῥόθος ἑλκομένης.
Hes.

ἐπιστάμενοι τὰ Λακ. φρονήματα ὡς ἄλλα φρονέοντων καὶ ἄλλα λεγόντων.
Herod.

89.

WHEN once you resign yourself to the
fancy that you "cannot help it"; when once
you let a phantasy of necessity jump on
your back and throw a bit into your jaws;
when you begin to breathe that impious
and blasphemous thought—then there is
no recklessness into which you are not
ready to plunge. That base and scheming
and miserable stroke of madness dashes
you aside from the right path. It is the
origin of what is evil to you, and makes
you bold for any wrong. Take care you
do not say, "I can't help it." Even if you
feel disposed to say it about little things
which are apparently irrelevant to morals,
you must suspect danger. Nothing with
which the will is concerned is irrelevant to
the moral life. Note the little speck within
your fruit, the little rift in the instrument
of your life's music. Will is Will whatever
be the matter on which it be called to work;
and if it is allowed to be weak in some small
thing to-day, the plague is begun, and it has
a precedent for avowing helplessness in
some greater thing to-morrow. He that

ἐπεὶ δ' ἀ-
νάγκας
ἔδυ λέπαδ-
νον κ.τ.λ.
Æsch.

Tennyson.

admits weakness in one point is potentially impotent in all. *Scelus intra se tacitè qui cogitat ullum Facti primum habet.* This will-weakness opens the door to indefinite crime. What but " *Thy* will be done" can secure us ? In the recognition of God's will as permanent within us is our strength found. It was not mock-humility, but sober common-sense and a clear perception of causes and sequences, which led that holy man to say when he saw a felon going to Tyburn, "But for the grace of God, there goes John Bradford."

90.

OH young man, leave not open the garden-gate of your heart for the swine to come in and trample down the flower-beds of the graces of your God.

91.

WHEN good men move about too much and pass to and fro among incitements to pleasure, it is as when a bottle of good wine gets shaken. The dregs and lees of the soul make the wine of life cloudy.

92.

ABSTRACT yourself for a moment, with your watch in your hand, from this beautiful order in which you live, and move, and are. Imagine yourself walking on the high places of heaven, in some place which is not as a place, some state or condition in which you can see the Universe lying at your feet. It is better thus to abstract yourself, for otherwise you form part of the argument, and this does not minister to lucidity. But say you see both in its broad working and in its delicate details of order and law, the Universe at your feet. Except you have carried with you the doubts of mortal questionists, would it not at once strike you that what you see *must* have come into existence as much by Will and purpose and Personal intervention as the watch which you hold in your hand? This is an old image, but it bears dwelling on. If that watch was contrived by a mind, so surely also was that Universe. Moreover, as *a man* constructed the parts of the watch, and brought them under the condition of the natural laws of motion, so it must have been Someone like man—or

Vivida vis animi pervi-cit et extra Processit longè flam-mantia mœnia mur-di; A:que omne immen-sum peragr-avit mente animoque, Unde refert nobis victor quid possit oriri. *Lucr.*

Tempus item per se non est. *Lucr.*

rather Someone to whom man is like—some Personage, that gave life within itself to the Universe as to one infinite living creature. And if this be true of the outside world of matter, shall not the observer, when he goes back again in thought to his own place in that Universe, argue much more clearly and certainly the same origin for himself, namely, a Personal Will? If a man dwells in the body of dust, and yet is not of it, so God, while independent of the Universe, may still be in it and give it life. God animates the body of the Universe, beings and all, just as a man's spirit, indivisible and invisible, animates the body of a man. The fact that the seen part of a man becomes unseen without, as we believe, carrying into death that part of him which has made the body seem for a time to have life in itself, looks like a prophecy that the "unseen Universe" will survive the Universe which is seen.

93.

FALSEHOOD can never *be* an aspect of truth.

94.

Ps. xxvii. 8.

PRAYER and its answer are, for instanta-
neous and exact response, like the voice and
its echo against that great Rock under which
we find shadow and shelter in this weary
land. The words of prevailing prayer come
back upon the soul in an answer of rejoicing
praise. "When I called, Thou didst answer:
and when I was yet speaking, Thou didst
hear." The reflection is however sometimes
clearer in the waters of the soul than that
which is reflected, and the echo sweeter than
the parent sound, mostly multiplying itself
with " re-sounding grace."

95.

IF an Inspector of spiritual meats were
to come round every Sunday, how many of
our Sermons would he pronounce fit for
human food (?) Postfix a query to this, or
not, according to your experience.

96.

IF willing in the day of our Maker's
power, much more shall we be willing in
the day of our Father's love.

Ro. xii. 2.

97.

BUSINESS is a kind of material body without which the spiritual life is a kind of ghost. In the perfect life they are essential to each other. Business, whatever attaches to each man's position, is dead if a man's spirit do not animate it. This spirit, however, if it have no body to animate, has but a shadowy life. So also material possession, or the fair power of obtaining food, raiment, and roof, forms that corporeal substance and local habitation, without which the spirit of love, however quick and fresh, is but an airy nothingness flying between the cold moon and the earth.

98.

PEOPLE who float a worldly enterprise by which they hope to gain advantage through the utilising of other people, commonly keep a private boat swinging astern.

99.

IN proportion as the truth makes men free, freedom will make men truthful.

100.

I WAS reading a book full of fine writing and vivid picturing, but every here and there I became aware of a smell of sulphur in it : something like the whiffs which puff before your nose and eyes as you are contemplating a beautiful view out of the window of a railway. No young person in these days should pick up books at haphazard. They should seek good advice as to what they read. He who said "Take heed how ye hear" would also say "Take heed how ye *read*." There may be moral death in those currents of bad air. The modesty of a life may wither in an hour.

101.

IF a man, through mistaken kindness, be elevated to great offices, and even though these offices involve dignity, emolument, and the *salutari, appeti, decedi, assurgi, deduci, reduci, consuli*, and the like honours— yet if, having some genuine and special gift, he finds in this post no scope to put it out to the Exchangers, he is not rightly happy, but is apt to be discontented and at last to flag.

102.

Would Christ have been called to die had He come earlier? It is hardly fair to say, "had He come among us now", for He has mainly made us what we are, a fact, by the way, which few of those delightful novelists who so delicately delineate our best phases and traits, have the grace and the candour to recognise. What would they themselves have been but for this Christian atmosphere? It would be an interesting field for enquiry to contemplate how the world might have been elevated into the nature of the New Man, if Christ, at His coming, *had* been received by His own Jews, and had He found human society so advanced as not to demand from Him the crucial test.

103.

If little sins have o'er thee taken hold,
Thine end, poor soul, is easy to be told.

104.

As to the pure all things are pure : so to the impure all things are impure. *Quantum in cælum, tantum in Tartara.*

105.

A BROKEN PEBBLE.

*   *   *

Then all the phases, told a thousand times
By tongue, or pen, or scene, yet ever new
And rife with interest to all that live :
For who that lives but knows some mood and
    tense,
Learned off by heart in this world's public
    school—
If not the present—*that* is best to know,
Most if indicative, no doubt subjoined—
Perhaps the Past, finished or still in course,
A preterite indefinite, with a hope—
Or, it may be, the Future, with a glance
Of foolish wisdom at the Future done—
All, all have learned, or else may come to learn,
Some mood and tense of that old verb, "*to love.*"

106.

BRING vividly before your mind any practical moral difficulty. The course of your probation, say, brings you into a certain crisis. These crises may be greater or less, but no crisis is unimportant. Such perplexities form part of the Holy War of our life. Every man has them more or less: and it is futile to say that your circumstances differ from those of other people ; nay, it is highly dangerous to say so, for your next step is to try and get out of your difficulty by some way by which other people's consciences do not allow them to get out of theirs. You are tempted to argue, "If my difficulty is an exception, my escape may perhaps also be excused if it be exceptional"; and that means *sin* : so put away at once and for ever the idea that your situation differs essentially from that in which most people are placed. You do· not know, and cannot guess, how many good Christians are manfully struggling through equal misfortune. Well—you want a solution, ease, rest ; in short, comfort. You desire to follow some particular course suited to your mind. It is natural you should wish thus, especially if that course be one in itself right; but does God make it right *for you?* This reservation is so important that it is wrong, however natural it may in this case seem, to desire anything except broadly and unreservedly God's will as expressed in His known commands. No man is in a safe or wholesome condition who writhes under his cross. The only wholesome tone of heart is, " Thy will be done; I desire nothing but Thine arrangement, O God my Father." This feeling, and nothing but this feeling working in the soul can draw us back, by the constraining love and grace of the Spirit of Christ and God, from the fearful gulfs of crime or death which lie between us and the objects to which we are drawn when we overstrongly desire a rest which our Father is not pleased to give us. Our rest must, I say, lie in the doing and abiding of God's will.

Miser, ah miser, querendum est etiam atque etiam, anime.

107.

THE fancifully jealous are not wise—
But yet 'twere foolish not to use thine eyes.

108.

IT is not so much that there may be this or that in the formularies of the Church really to object to, but the fact is that there is, and always will be, a certain amount of combativeness in every country and every place; and the Church, occupying a prominent position, comes in for all random buffets of those who like to exercise their thews in laying about them. This has done the Church no little good. In a gymnasium there is a buffer which men strike with their fists, in order to test and improve their strength by trying to drive it in as hard as they can. The men who thus practise get stronger, and it does not do the leather any harm. I have gone into a gymnasium for many years, and the same old bit of leather stands where it did, and the spring has not a whit been weakened. When it becomes limp, it can be renovated. Dissent, or rather an undue continuance of dissent, in part owes its vitality to a morbid vigour in the temper of the land; to something in the British Lion which *must* have something to hit at. There are some people whose irritability of constitution drives them to keep busy with tongue or pen. Good and wise men in this case do useful or harmless work. Dissent and the like tempers in the State have had just and solid reasons in their origin, and now go on by habit, owing mainly to the organisation of systems, which bring bread to Ministers and custom to the chapel-shops, long after their *raison d'être* has ceased ; as wheels go on after the strap is off, or as limbs twitch when no longer in connection with the nervous centres. I have seen a duck waddle on when its head was off. Also men of spiritual convictions and conscious of power must have range for work, and they are bound by the vigour of their new nature to speak the things they do know and testify of what their inner eye has seen. At present they are the right men in the wrong places ; but the Church to which there still holds the name of England can find ample room and verge enough for all such to help her to trace the characters of heaven.

ἔκνιζέ μ' αἰεὶ τοῦτο. *Soph.*

Mutatoque ordine mutant Naturam. *Lucr.*

Revocate Parentem. *Verg.*

Amor mi mosse, che mi fa parlare *D.*

109.

" I WILL at once set my will to work to resist this desire of being idle." What is the *I* here? Is "*I*" the will itself? or is it an " I " behind the will? or again, is it a name given to the parts of the being at different times, as each comes forward in dominance or prominence? or does it represent the composite being? If this last be the case, then you mean that the whole of you, namely *you*, will set to work, or set your will to work to resist that part of you which desires to be idle? But in this case the part which desires to be idle will take part with "you" in your whole against itself as a part, and set the will to work against itself! This will not hold. So does the matter resolve itself to a struggle between you and this desire? Desire says, "You shall not set will to work to keep me down." But your very complaint is, that desire is an overpowering element in you. Desire bribes and buys up the will; οὐκ ἀδέκαστοι κρίνομεν say Aristotle and St. James. We have not found what, behind the overpowered will, is the " I " that can renew its strength. Does not "I" mean the divine Sovereign Power whom I recognise in my island of life, and in virtue of which I partake of the Divine Nature? Therefore do you not mean to say "I will, in God's name, set in motion the human agency, namely my will, to subdue that rebel desire?" Thus is it that the voice of God speaks within you. What, I should like to know, is a man to do, who does not recognise that Power resident in his life, when under the superhuman strain of a conjuncture of temptations? What is left him but to fall? Lord, to whom shall we go? Thou only hast the words of eternal life.

110.

I WONDER why a certain class of persons, or rather of parsons, make such a dead set against *feeling*. Is it simply lest people should be misled? I fear it is connected with the dislike of letting people know that they are forgiven, a knowledge which of course fills men with joy. If people know they are forgiven, they can do without human intervention, and the occupation of the *sacerdos* is gone. *Voilà tout.*

Possunt quia posse videntur. *Verg.*

Dis carus ipsis. *Hor.*

Io son fatta da Dio, sua mercè, tale Che la vostra miseria non me tange. *D.*

My son, give me thy heart. GOD.

III.

WHAT will the material world die of? what but decay of Nature? If parts of the world die—and what represents the death or rather the slumber of matter, if Greenland and the Sahara do not?—it is obvious, the whole world may die in its body; or at least fall into sleep, the twin-brother of death, θανάτῳ ἄγχιστα ἐοικώς. Paralysis of limbs has gone on for some time; the power of lush gigantic production has largely subsided, and we are told the sun tends to grow cold. Growth is clearly setting in a spiritual and away from a material direction. What the world now looks to is "seed of men and growth of mind" and spirit. Yet when we see its most advanced Sovereign State wish in the madness of toleration to abnegate its charter of Dominion, and to throw away the Christ-Nature to any chance passer-by that may choose to spoil it, we cannot but feel with alarm that the world's Mind is terribly deranged. This is because it foregoes its arranged place under the Spirit. The future Universe in the fining process seems likely in due course to coalesce with

τοὐπιόν-
τος'
ἁρπάσαι
Soph.

Quapropter,
quamvis
caussando
multa mo-
reris, Esse

and to be gathered up into the Unseen. in rebus in-
ane tamen
fateare ne-
cesse est.
Lucr. As for its matter, why should not this fall off from its Spirit, as the body of its microcosmic man from his? or has the Poet thereof prepared no glorified body for the whole, as for the part?

112.

IN cities see we more the works of men,
In fields the purer works of God we ken ;
But yet, with hand or mind do all he can,
'Tis God who does all works done well by man.

113.

WE must not make anything, even peace and a wholesome moral atmosphere, however much to be desired, a *sine quâ non* in our demands on Providence. We must not vainly imagine any demands at all, but we Vuolsi cosl
colà, dove si
puote Cio
che si vuole,
e piu non
dimandare.
D. must preserve a *tabula rasa* of all our personal wishes or inclinations. We must find our only rest in the attitude of " Thy will be done," and thus calmly face whatever demands upon our action or our endurance the solemn hours and the holy moments may bring us.

114.

EXCEPT principle, there ought to be nothing hard and fast in humanity. All rules relating to our dealing therewith ought to fit to it like a Coan vest; our rules ought to enswathe it as the atmosphere invests the earth. The free play of the winds of feeling ought to curve our conduct about all its beautiful forms, lest they be hidden and cramped. We are not dealing with necessary matter, nor with things always demanding or admitting rigid demonstration or fixed application; we must measure at least many human cases with a μολυβδίνη κανών, showing all the curves of their waved moulding; not so much with inflexible justice as with the equity of common feeling; with that equity which, as one has well said, is not better than justice, but a better justice. Fair play is indeed a jewel.

115.

Lasciami andar, chè nel cielo è voluto. *Dante.*

A DYING lady said to her friends praying round her, "How good it is of you all to help me on to glory."

116.

IT is one of the largest, most interesting, and most practical questions, how the parts of the life may co-operate. It should be a standing topic for preachers ; but it requires the utmost wisdom and delicacy. It embraces all gospel teaching. Men in possession of the seed of the Christ-Spirit may convert souls, which is the first and main thing, but to guide the details of the Christian life, and to treat cases of conscience, surely requires also the highest culture.

117.

IT is most unwise to let ourselves be brought to anchor by any gloomy thoughts. Anybody may do so who is mad enough for it. Reckon over the things that have happened to you, except you have been unusually fortunate, in the last ten or twenty years, and you may in ten or twenty minutes come to regard yourself as the most ill-used creature on the face of the earth. Losses of goods, real or personal, in all senses of the words—repeated failures and countless disappointments—why, if you contemplate

Genti, che
l'aer nero si
gastiga.
Dante.

these "in the lump," and these only, your future catches the same tinge, and then in what a black atmosphere may you imagine yourself to be living! But it is an untrue estimate. "Forget those things which are behind, and reach forth to those things which are before." Is not the whole of hope and the whole of Heaven before you? Never dream that Heaven need be among the things that are left behind you and lost. Be not faithless, but believing, and then all happiness is *before* you and lies yet within your reach. You may yet be " more than conqueror through Him that loves you to the end."

118.

On one bad thought whoever broods within,
Hath the prime movement of the glaring sin.

119.

If a Christian is ill—he is ill unto the Lord. It is as active work to suffer God's will as to do it. The soul, like the deponent verb, then wears a passive form, but has an active meaning.

120.

THOSE who would alter in their mind the law of God to suit their pleasures or weaknesses, are like those who change the fingers of the clock, or think to put back the wheels of the sun, to make themselves in time ; as though in either case eternal movements or eternal institutions could be changed, or in any way affected or stayed in their calm round.

ὧν νόμοι πρόκεινται ὑψίποδες.
Soph.

121.

THOSE who are aggressive are commonly retrogressive, and not progressive. Progress is indeed aggress, but it is aggressive only upon ignorance and darkness. All time spent in aggressiveness upon our honest fellowmen is lost to progress, and, as we cannot stand still, we are at such times retrogressive.

122.

PEOPLE often confuse the casual and the causal. In fact nothing is casual. The best definition of chance is " the absence of known cause."

οὐκ ἐστὶ τῶν πόλλων ἑταιρεῖν καὶ διορίζειν.
Arist.

123.

LET every day be to thee a day of judgment. Get the scrutinizing, and trutinising mercy of the Most High to examine thy thoughts day by day, to cleanse thee from thy secret faults, and to lead thee into the land of uprightness. Thou wilt meet the Great Day well if thou get the Great Judge to judge thee every day.

124.

FRIEND, art thou fain to lead a quiet life?
Put up with much before thou plunge in strife.

125.

WE best show our regard for character by the character of our regard.

126.

Ὦ
τἀληθὲς
ἐμπέφυ-
κεν
ἀνθρώπων
μόνῳ.
Soph.

REMEMBER that Jesus, "the same yesterday, to-day, and for ever," is not responsible for any foolish things which the Church and the Churches—still less for what wayward and irresponsible individuals—from time to time may have said, may be saying, or yet may say.

127.

A REAL grievance is the only grist for the mill of discontent. If the grindstones have nothing between them, they grind themselves smooth ; and then, and not till then, will the sound of the grinding be low. If they get an imagined grievance between them, "the common sense of most," which soon sees through a millstone, leaves the business to a few ; and the character of these is soon added up, and they are not long in wearing themselves out. A wise legislator will keep removing one after another all reasons for indignation, and all temptations and facilities for wrong deeds and for wild and whirling words ; and will, by degrees, still the noise of national waves and the madness of the people. Easy-going persons generally complain of nothing when there is nothing to complain of.

128.

WARE, as a rule, the bearing of a tale ;
But where to tell were just, thou must not fail.

129.

SILENCE does *not* give consent.

Muta metu.
Lucr.

130.

BE careful how you regard your neighbour's character. With all his low habits he is, for aught you know, contending against them more sincerely, and making head against them more effectually, than you are against those which may beset yourself. No one knows the things of a man, save the spirit of a man which is in him, and—He who knows what is in man, and Who is the Judge of quick and dead. Not but what there are those who must at once be known by their fruits; thistles, from which it is plain that no man can ever gather figs.

131.

HOWEVER this or that nation or generation of the Society of men may deal with their own hopes and chances of salvation, God's Kingdom must come, and the Communion of Saints must go on. " Heaven and earth shall pass away, but My word shall not pass away."

132.

SOLIDITY is often confused with *stolidity*, and *vice versâ*.

133.

I FOUND in an old desk a love-letter that never
went, from a departed one to one long ago departed ;

I saw the image of a day-moon on a running
stream;

I saw the shadow of a cloud upon a cloud ;

I dreamed a dream about a dream.

σκιᾶς ὄναρ

The φαντασία of Epictetus is, as Mr.
George Long tells us, not only the thing
perceived, but the impression which it
makes; which latter is therefore an appearance of an appearance! And such are
the things which war against our souls, and
lure us into the whirlpools! "Our Babe"
may well have power to control this crew
of wonderfully pale spectres.

Simillima
proles.   *V.*

134.

English Priest. Why do you do ministerial work in my parish?

Nonconformist Minister. Because my Directory found souls there whom nobody else got at. Being constrained by the love of Christ, and wishing to devote my life to bringing souls to Him, I offered myself for the work.

E.P. But now *I* am come to get at those souls.

N.M. But your Church is, as we see, not always sure to send men who will care, or will be able, to get at them. Perhaps you are mistaken in thinking *you* can get at them. It is perhaps only men of my class who can do so.

E.P. Then will you remain at work under my direction?

N.M. It is too late to ask that, for I am under an organisation by means of which I truly labour to win bread for my children—much as, I suppose, you do for yours.

E.P. Then I must either regard you (1) as an enemy, or (2) with indifference, or (3) as my helper in the main, and as

οὐ γάρ τι
σοι ζῶ
δοῦλος
ἀλλὰ
Λοξίᾳ.
Soph.

οὐδέ κασί-
γνητος φί-
λος ἔσσε-
ται ὡς τὸ
πάρος
περ, αἶψα
δὲ γηράσ-
κοντας
ἀτιμήσου-
σι τοκῆας.
Hes.

building up with me the invisible, while
pulling down from me a visible Church.
(1) I cannot regard you as an enemy, for
you try and make my people, at least
these people, good. (2) For the same
reason I cannot regard you with indifference. (3) Lastly, and for the same reason
still, I must regard you as my friend, if you
will let it be so ; and I hope you may
regard me as yours. I shall be thankful to
you, except your organisation demands it,
not to have your meetings in Church hours ;
and, except your conscience demands it, not
to say things against my work. I, for my
part, must strive to maintain the beauty of
true Unity, and the wrong of needless
schism ; but I shall pay due regard to con-
stitutional freedom, and shall rather maintain our own position than assail yours.
If you cannot settle down with me on this
understanding, then I can only say, " The
Lord be judge between us." Now let us
pray. Let me ask you to begin.

μάντιν
οὕτινα
ψέγων.
Æsch.

οὐκ ἐρῶ
Φοίβου γ'
ἀπ' αὐτοῦ
τῶν δ'
ὑπηρετῶν
δ' ἄπο.
Soph.

" Imports
thy loss be-
yond the pre-
sent need ?"
Lady. " No
less than if I
should my
brothers
lose."
Milton.

135.

I WILL not grieve that I am thus bereft,
But think how ill I merit what is left.

136.

IF you have an interest in your mind and are still training it, I should advise you, after you have been reading about a matter, to ask yourself before you dismiss it—first, what you have read that is worth making a part of your knowledge : then, whether you have really made it a part thereof. To a reading age, the same Voice that said "For every idle word that men shall speak" would, I think, have said, not only, "For every idle word that men and women shall write," but also "For every idle book that men and women, and youths and maidens shall *read*, they shall give account thereof in the day of judgment." In this matter of light literature the Enemy, be it well known, is very busy in sowing Tares. Every maiden should, and every young lady will, take the advice of competent judges before plunging into converse, for so it is, with authors and authoresses. If they do not take care, the reading of an hour may poison the sweetness, and wither the beauty of a life.

Quella lettura scolorocci il viso : * * * più non vi leggemmo avante. *D.*

137.

IT is important not to contemplate with the mind's eye the wrong pleasure, while it is important to contemplate rather with the spirit's eye the great gulf fixed between that false pleasure and your true. That gulf may seem narrow, or it may seem to be no gulf at all; but·once leap at those dangerous flowers which hang there, and, probably immediately, certainly ere long, you will find yourself, with their few leaves in your hot hands, tumbling headlong into the abyss.

138.

To cure is well; 'tis better to prevent:
That proves thee potent, but this provident.

139.

WE stand now over some of the mysteries of Eternity as children that look with fear down into deep, dark ponds on winter evenings. On some eternal summer-day we may pass that way and find them dried to the abiding ground, and the mystery at an end.

Guarda,
e passa. *D.*

140.

WHEN setting out upon a journey we take much thought and make much preparation. We think of where we are going to, how we shall get there, what will be needed for the way, what dangers are to be encountered, what difficulties to be overcome, what companions we shall take with us, and lastly, what requisites there are for our comfortable continuance when we get to our journey's end and to the place where we would be. In all these respects the wise man will look to his passage over the space of time, how wide or how narrow soever, which lies between the present moment and that of "quick-coming death." Lord of heaven and earth, to Whom the wise all aspire, in whose light Jesus, my Master, lived and lives, guide me by Thy counsel, and after that receive me—I dare not say with glory, but with mercy.

141.

θρίξ ἀνὰ
μέσσον.

IT requires care, both in State and Church, to keep defence from looking like defiance.

142.

CAIAPHAS and the rest were probably many of them "well meaning" men, "firm" men, men not easily disturbed from their prejudices ; they were men of "settled convictions," "steady principles," "cautious men"—in a word, what some unreflecting people love to call "sound Churchmen." Their sin was that they thought they saw. They simply regarded reconsideration to be a sin ; and, this being a thought of foolishness, they remained in the ,sin of not reconsidering. So they tried to put out the Light. The same sin keeps men now from seeing Who Christ really is. The Saviour is thus crucified in the Spirit over and over again, in all circles, high and low. Indeed, the best are only feeling after Him, if haply they may find Him.

Put out the light, and then—put out The Light.
Shaks.

143.

LIKE one that stands in the glow of the sunset, so, washed in the light of Christ, we lose much local colour. In Thy light we shall not only see light but *be* light. "Be ye light in the Lord."

ἐν οὐρανῷ
κάλλισ-
τον
κελάδημα
Eur.

144.

SEQUESTERED from the crew, as best they may,
In sunny nook beside the breezy prow,
By use of voyage made familiar now,
How sweet through all the long Atlantic day,
Neath the broad heaven's shadow-shifting brow
To list the changeful waters in their play;
Which falling off in furrows leave a way,
While the winds chaunt as only they know how:
Thrice blest to gaze into each others' eyes,
In idle interval of destinies,
And read, as in the volume of a book,
Trust and dependence there in every look;
To make each other's breast by turns a pillow,
And dream of golden homes beyond the billow.

145.

So love the twain, as only those can know,
Who, winged as seeds upon the westward wind,
The blue above them and the green below,
Fare forth with resolute heart and even mind,
Before them ocean, home and friends behind.
They know not rightly to what land they go,
But this at least they know—that Heaven is
    kind.
And Faith and Hope and Love endear them so,
As none can tell but two such souls as they,
And more than e'en their own sweet sense can
    say.
The uncertain sea their only known abode,
They lean each on the other, both on God ;
And all the fret and change of this world's
    weather
But twine their twiune fates more fast together.

146.

THAT which gives authority in the utter-
ance of something just and right, or merciful
and faithful, is, not the adopting of this
or that formula, but the expression of the
moral sense upon its own knowledge and
responsibility. "We speak that we do
know." This tells with natural force, arrests
the attention, bites the heart. We feel that
we are being addressed out of Eternity.
We hear, as Chateaubriand somewhere has
it, the sound of something falling from
heaven.

147.

CHILDREN should be given the keys of
all knowledge, and the chief ingredients of
things. They should be put in possession
of main ideas in accordance with the most
approved discoveries, typical specimens of
all the best human utterances, and the
elements of wit and humour. Each mental
form should be rightly channelled out. It
is surely a great omission not to teach in a
simple practical manner, if only in illustra-
tive conversations, the laws of thought :—I

do not say they need study Trendelenburg,
or the Posterior Analytics. But in all,
through all, and above all they should have
their hearts engraven with the highest laws
of morals, and should be taught God,
Christ, and the Holy Spirit in the conscience. If not, they remain low animals,
with the dangerous addition of intelligence
for sin.

148.

I ONCE saw a little child try to wheel a
small donkey-cart : the cart, to his surprise
and joy, went on at a rapid pace ; and the
child crowed with pride. It did not see
that its father had given it a good push
from behind. The father did not spoil the
child's exultation by disabusing it of the
illusion ; but it was a very little child, and
of no great wit.

149.

WITH some, prayer and praise are, too
often, no more and no less than when men
say "bless your life" and "good-bye,"—
which latter often means "go to the—crows."

150.

τήνῳ τὰ
σὰ δάκρυα
μᾶλα
ῥέοντι.
Hes.

Thinking of the authority of the Master of the College, and forgetting the possible influence of a Tutor of that . College, a father took his poor boy out of the way of what he fancied to be the Scylla of Liberality, but flung him incontinently into what was the raging Charybdis of mental licentiousness ; much like a woman who breaks a delicate vase while moving it nervously away from where she fears it may be broken.

151.   .

αἰεὶ δ᾿ ἀμ-
βολιεργὸς
ἀνὴρ
ἄτῃσι
παλαίει.
Hes.

ONE of the most uncomfortable marks of disorder in the life is, when a man so ill divides his time that undone duties clamour at him whenever he would enjoy some otherwise legitimate leisure and some otherwise refreshing pleasure.

152.

All skirts ex-
tended of thy
mantle hold.
Trench.

ALWAYS listen intently to any sane man who can tell you what God hath done for his soul. There is no topic of such exciting and such abiding interest. You are there face to face with eternal verities.

153.

IT is wonderfully touching to see how an old man sometimes gives forth his utterances in a spirit which seems independent of whether the hearers hearken. He is less capable of the ἔχθιστη ὀδύνη. He has lost indeed the *fervor juventæ* : he does not now, as he once did, press what he has to say with gesture and eye ;—but take note, he speaks more like a voice dropping from somewhere above us.

Torpent in-
fractæ ad
prœlia vires.
Verg.

Ἄρης δ'
οὐκ ἔνι
χώρᾳ.
Æsch.

Πόλυ
γλυκίων
μελίτος
ῥέεν αὔδη.
Hom.

154.

IF you look at a wheat-field from all ways but one, it will seem to you disordered, and you will not be able to judge of its culture or its produce. But if you move along till you can glance up the rows of the drill, all starts into order. How much depends on the point of view from which we regard things.

155.

THE outside must play its part in the most important arrangements. If fools exaggerate, they are also fools who ignore this.

159.

WHILE mighty masters of music and poetry are studying all the laws of art, threading the myriad mazes of harmony, toiling away to fulfil their capacities and make themselves a name, lo and behold a sweet spirit of wild beauty comes from black lips and takes the country by storm. These songs from the rice-grounds of Carolina seem to retain an overmastering charm, though representing the lives and the loves of slaves. Thus it has also been in Religion. While Bishops and Deans, Archdeacons and Canons, not to say the rural Deans, and all regular and irregular Ministers, are elaborately endeavouring to consolidate or adorn the edifice of Christianity, lo and behold, a common, uncultured, kindly, nasal man, with a single singer of affecting doggrel, steps on our shores, and becomes the channel of infusing into our English society a new flood of spiritual life, of which Princesses, and Legislators, and Ministers both of State and Church press to drink. At a time when many of our best Churches are turned into Theatres, Moodie turns one of our best Theatres into a Church, as though it had been burnt, emptied, and swept of all its *vilis supellex* for the express convenience of this messenger of God. The great Church-preacher of the day praises God for him in the University pulpit, and the children of the people, taken with the sweet spirit of his holy hymns, waken the households—make the streets and lanes of the cities and towns, at all odd hours, ring again with their jubilant Hosannas—and, taking the soul of waste places, flood village and field all over with eddying song. Thus, out of the mouths of babes and sucklings, from Moodie up to these, God perfects praise ; and thus the weak things of the world confound the wise—except where the wise are wise enough to see which way that wind blows, and are not so mad but they can tell a hawk from a "heronsew."

> Hinc nova proles Artu-bus infirmeis teneras lasciva per herbas ludit lacte mero mentes per-culsa novel-las. *Lucr.*

160.

ONE man accuses, another excuses, every-body—except himself. The latter is the more graceful character, but "*est modus in rebus.*"

> Qui s'excuse s'accuse.

161.

CATERPILLARS, accustomed to one leaf, have been known to die rather than eat of another. I am informed that in the times before the flood of '48 a little German principality used to kill its criminals by giving them nothing but veal and red wine. (I grant that my informant was a Republican.) It is clear that there is much that is morbid, as well as something that may be wholesome, about the desire in some of us to live upon the teaching of some one person, and so to assume his colour at the loss of our own. God hath said, "of every tree of the garden thou mayest freely eat— *except one.*" Some people so entirely pervert the right way of the Lord, that they are wont to eat only of that one. They surely die.

They shall go in and out, and find pasture.
CHRIST.

162.

THE Gospel bids us be single eyed,—but not one-eyed.

'Twere better to pluck out one eye, 'tis true,
Than having two to enter into Hell :—
But then to enter Heaven having two,
The Lord, methinks, would say were just as well.

163.

WITH a man of great family and noble blood, these accidents—if indeed they are accidents, and if they do not enter into the composition of the man—are only ridiculous if he exhibits undue consciousness thereof. Everybody in his senses must surely note that " noble blood " is of a nature to be a blessing. To come of a race guarded through successive generations from the corroding causes which accompany need ; never to have had the flame of genius repressed, nor the genial currents of the family soul frozen by penury ; always to have had engrained in the stock the delicate sensibilities and the kindly traditions of a studious civility ; to inherit the fine feeling and the high honour which, wherever else it may be found, has mostly become a second nature in such a family tree ; to have enjoyed, under wise tuition, from childhood up, constant supplies of mental food, as furnished by the library of a great and good house ; to have fed on the cream of the best literature of all time past and present ; to have had free access to the splendid inspirations of

Δεινὸς
χαρακτὴρ
κἀπίση-
μος ἐν
βροτοῖς
Ἐσθλῶν
γενέσθαι,
κἀπὶ μεῖ-
ζον ἔρχε-
ται τῆς
εὐγενείας
ὄνομα
τοῖσιν
ἀξίοις.
Eur.

ἔχει γε
μεντοι
καὶ τὸ
θρεφθῆ-
ναι καλῶς
δίδαξιν
ἐσθλόν.
Eur.

εἴπερ τις
ἄλλος
πιστὸς
·ὡς νομεὺς
ἀνήρ.

οὐδ' ἄν εἰ
τρίτης
ἐγὼ μη-
τρὸς φανῶ
τρίδουλος
Soph.

the poets and the keen precepts of the best moralists ; to have assimilated the forth-flowings of the sublimest oratory; above all, to have learned to cherish noble traditions of the history at once of his family and his country ; to own forefathers who have worked, and fought, and bled in the best causes ; lastly, to have been born and bred to the manner of high-minded statesmanship—I can only say that the man who calls all that nothing must be a fool. Not but what it holds quite true that, if a man with all these antecedents be not in the Kingdom of Heaven, the least in that Kingdom, though he have none of them, is better off than he.

164

"REDIT os placidum moresque benigni,
Et venit ante oculos et pectore vivit imago."

[Quoted by Professor Sedgwick at a meeting in the University of Cambridge, in proposing a memorial for the Prince Consort.]

Those kindly ways, that gentle face,
　　On all our memories rise ;
His image in our heart holds place,
　　And lives before our eyes.

165.

MUCH may be learnt from dwelling on the right mode of nourishing the mental life, as to the best mode of nourishing the spiritual life. However much may be learned from analogy in the general regions of life outside our composite nature, still more is likely to be learned where both ratios, as here the mental and spiritual, lie close in the same subjective range. The reason why well-drawn arguments from wisely chosen analogies have a presumption in their favour and connote probability in their conclusions—connote, that is, a probable advancing towards truth, according to the amount of agreement and resemblance in the ratios under contemplation—is, that God is One. He pervades Being. His laws are uniform. Thus, whatever we look at, we may—I do not say think it likely that God has a hand in it, but feel sure that God is at the bottom of it, and that these uniform laws of His are at work. We perceive one and the same Spirit under diversities of operations. For instance, if I am regarding the relation of a mother country towards her colonies as one ratio; and if I seek to draw some argument for due treatment of these colonies from noting resemblances between the mother country with her colonies for one ratio, and the parent of a family with her children as my other ratio; when I have once established certain fair resemblances, and found the comparison of my ratios to be legitimate, as both being instances and parts of the one progressive line of human advance; when, that is, I have found that the relation between the individual unit and its offshoots finds its larger development in the national unit and its offshoots :—it gives me, I say, a firmer ground for my analogical argument, to remember that both a parent and a nation own the same Life-source of Humanity, and that so I may expect to find the same law running through both. It only remains for me to be careful that my inferences be limited *ratione similitudinis.* I am, moreover, more likely to find truth when the ratios have both to do with one fundamental idea, namely in this case the on-working of humanity, than if one of my ratios had been drawn, say, from the relation of a fowl to its chicks, or a parent-pea to its pods.

This being so in the case which I have instanced, much more, I repeat, is it likely that true lessons will be learned from an analogy when both ratios lie within a narrower compass still, and nestle more closely under the law, not only of general but individual humanity. The spirit with its receptivities lives with the same body in which resides the mind with *its* receptivities, these being

> "Three sisters,
> That doat upon each other," parts of "man,
> Living together under the same roof,
> And never can be sundered without tears."

Again, since the mind in its nature lies closer to the spirit than the body does, therefore analogies in which the spirit and the *mind* enter into the same compared ratios are likely to have more resemblances even than analogies in which the *body* and the spirit enter into the two ratios ; though many lessons, and often the same, may be learnt also from these.

What I have said has, I hope, been clearing the ground for the following remark. *The spirit stands to its food as the mind to its food.* Now we observe that the mind, like the body in that, thrives upon food convenient for it. The more just thoughts of an intellectual nature the mind has, the more sound books it eats, the more argument it practises, and the more it converses with reasonable men, the stronger, more active and more rich it grows. And even though it may never reproduce the facts it learns, nor ever repeat the forms of argument it has fed on, yet, from the exercise it has and from the habits it forms, it is more fit to grapple with the difficulties that present themselves. Now so it obviously must be with the *spirit* of man. What is the food of the spirit? *The things of the Spirit,* above all the Word of God; holy thoughts, wise sayings, high principles, and the converse of the sane people of God. The more it feeds on these, the stronger it is, the loftier it is, the purer it is. What makes the spirit weak and sickly among us, and why do our spirits sometimes seem to fall into the sleep of death? It is from not taking enough of wholesome food; from not reading or hearing the Word of God more; from not dwelling on the love of God and the Saviour more; from not quenching our thirst more at the divine fountains, but rather quenching the Spirit by whom our Spiritual thirst can alone be quenched; from not in joyful regularity nourishing our conscience more with heavenly moni- tions; from not praying more, and not watching more unto prayer. This it is which alone can keep down the lower desires. If we walked in the Spirit more, we should fulfil the desires of the flesh and of the mind less. Our spirits, in fine, like our minds and like our bodies, grow thin, withered, gaunt, and emaciated, from not feeding more freely on that which is alone their natural diet. " *He that eateth me, even he shall live by me.*"

Sic omnia debent Dis- solvi, simul ac cessârit suppeditari Materies.
Lucr.

John vi. 57.
CHRIST.

166.

IF any reader ignores the spiritual region, I fling him that last pebble, and others, to play with—much as I would to my dear dog.

A pocket

167.

MANY a man, in fact most Christians, can stand up before God and say, "Here am I, by Thy grace, at this moment better, stronger, and more hopeful than ever in my life. Those perils, which Thou hast helped me to face, those dreaded evils which Thou hast helped me to stem, are all to me now like a dream when one awakes. The blessings I have gained form a part of my eternal soul; the miseries I have suffered have absolutely vanished. So, strengthened by this experience, I am ready to turn over

Frui paratis et valido mihi, Latoe, dones. *Hor.*

any fresh page in my life. Only do Thou make my way plain before my face, even though it be only a little before the time for action, or only in that hour. Help me to trust Thee, even though with pain Thou shalt sever my spirit from my dust." Yet there is no more solemn ἀλαλητόν στέναγμα, no more hardly uttered groan, in all our formularies than that in the Service for the Burial of the dead, in which we pray "Thou knowest, Lord, the secrets of our hearts; shut not Thy merciful ears to our prayer; but spare us, Lord most holy, O God most mighty, O holy and merciful Saviour, Thou most worthy Judge Eternal, suffer us not, at our last hour, for any pains of death, to fall from Thee." The extraordinary earnestness of this prayer seems startling to those who are familiar with triumphant departures; but it suits the solemnity of the occasion, and who of us dare hesitate to adopt it ?

168.

MARRIAGES for beauty or for wit are like those beach-residences, which, being built as summer-houses for passing lodgers, give but a windy shelter to one who tries to live in them through the wild winter.

Sævo cum joco. *Hor.*

169.

Lo, from first to last, willy-nilly man ;
What he wills he cannot, will not what he can.

170.

TOLERATION perpetrates suicide when she tolerates within herself a powerful Intoleration, which is backed up by all the worst and strongest weaknesses of humanity.

171.

WHEN the Scripture says "I suppose
the world itself would not contain the books
that should be written," the expression,
except indeed it be a mere loose hyperbole,
seems to utter a sense of that which has
already almost come about. Have not the
few seeds of Christ's remembered words
already multiplied into an almost infinite
crop of books? And do they not still show
such a geometric proportion of fertility that
few libraries can hope to garner all the truths
of life and immortality which He is bringing
to light by His Gospel? No man, however
clear his mind and retentive his memory,
can profess to grasp and retain the whole
range of that which is worth knowing in
Theology; to say nothing of those other
ranges of knowledge to which the Truth that
makes men free is constantly giving rise.
This interpretation makes it no hyperbole to
say what the Scripture says; indeed one
cannot conceive that the writer, except he
simply adopted a common expression, should
have had anything else in his mind. There
can be no other idea attached to the words

save that which I have noted ; namely, that in the mental and spiritual capacity and receptivity of the world, the solution of the Christ-nature would become more than saturate. What marvellous fecundity there is in the Divine words! I know of a country-parson, to take one out of hundreds of like instances, who has a small library full of Theological things well said, but he hardly has time to absorb and use them. Why ? Because, in pondering merely the great Christian documents, he has so many things to say, which flow from his own narrow personal experience of the infinite application of those few sayings of His Master. Thus every one who comes to know any thing of Christ finds that his own little world cannot contain the things that have been, and might be written.

172.

Oh Maker of our brother-band,
O Lover and Support of all—
Of what should fall let nothing stand ;
Of what should stand let nothing fall.

173.

LOGICIANS, though incidentally right as to fact, are logically wrong in defining man as "a rational animal." If, moreover, in defining man, "animal" were justly limited by "rational," they ought to say, "man is *the* rational animal," though indeed even thus they might still say, "*a* man is a rational animal," meaning that he is *one* of the rational animals. I remark, however, that they are incidentally right in saying man is *a* rational animal, though not in *defining* man as such ; for "rational" covers most of organic creation. Yet to say, "man is *the* rational animal" would be correct as a definition, if the word "rational" were synonymous with "devotional." But this they do not mean. The difference between beast and man may almost be put by describing one as a preying animal, and the other as an animal that can pray.

Dominion in the head and breast.
Tenn.

174.

THOSE alone do not believe in God who do not know Him. Belief increases with knowledge, and knowledge with belief.

Hos. vi. 3.

175.

[*To the dinner-table of the aged Mother of the Coningtons.*]

THOU fine-grained square, whose tinct of ebony
Our handmaids chafe to radiance as of old,
How many faces of the past in thee
My trance-fed soul is bending to behold !
What polished quips, what fruits of thought,
 what glee,
What clear-cut tales thy mirror might unfold ;
Thy memory might upserve what pleasantry
Of genial gossip, were the store outrolled :
I see the same bright ball above thee shine,
Whose image then thy magic glass down-took,
The lamp that lit those lineaments, divine
Because on Jesu's face, we trust, they look :—
As the moon, clear-set in yon heavenly land,
Repeats herself far down in sea-left sand.

Boston,
  September 20th, 1873.

176.

THE very sense of "honour," the very claims of "family," the very desire "to take a commanding position," "to be admitted to the best society," and the like considerations, will, if I mistake not, render it ere long impossible for most people, who have any sense and any self-respect, to remain old creatures in the first Adam, when it is open to them to become new creatures in our second, the A and Ω of Humanity. Darwin is doing good service to the Type of the NEW MAN.

177.

BLESSED are they that mourn. They that take sorrow jauntily, or who amidst work, pleasure, society, or change, seek to quench thought and feeling and forget their loss, are not blessed in their grief. It is not well to forget the loss of those whom we love, but rather to remember it rightly.

178.

WHEN we lose one we love, let us learn to love the more ONE we cannot lose.

179.

WHAT new and pure delight will open upon the soul, when he enters his new abode, and the angels begin to show him some of the beauties that are there—such pleasures at least as he is capable of in that new infancy of his being. How pleasant it is, when we go into a fresh country, or a neighbourhood grander and more sublime than our own, and take in new ideas. We stand with uplifted eyes in moods of attentive rapture, amidst the vallies and mountains that wind away and rise to Heaven; or if we go into the Capitals and wander among the galleries and the treasures, every step we take enlarges our ideas of beauty and our standard of wealth. And much more, we trust, will it be so in an infinitely higher range, when we, by the great grace of God, find ourselves in the better country, that is in the Heavenly.

180.

χαρά μ' ὑφέρπει δάκρυον ἐκκαλουμένη.
A joy steals o'er me calling out a tear.

οἱ γὰρ
ἔμπειροι
περὶ ἕκασ-
τα κρίν-
ουσιν
ὀρθῶς τὰ
ἔργα καὶ
δι' ὧν ἢ
πῶς ἐπι-
τελεῖται
συνιᾶσιν
καὶ ποῖα
ποίοις
συνᾴδει.
Arist.

181.

CHRIST'S main command is that we pray to God. If a man do not keep this main command, how can he know that he knows God? The part which is best in him, τὸ κράτιστον ἐν αὐτῷ as Aristotle has it, goes on in darkness. All his foundations are out of course. Are those men who do not even know the highest life to be *judges* of that life? Is their authority to be taken against its reality? What can be more preposterous? I do not want to press matters too far home, but you may depend upon it that these men do not pray. God's wind in due course shall blow them and their inanities into the blackness of darkness.

182.

ST. JOHN, when he wrote to his readers as his " children," wrote from the high position of one who had leaned, and still was leaning, on the breast of Christ. The new man is in the highest degree philoprogenitive. Who would not long to bring many sons to glory?

183.

THE dogs move about among a set of ideas and facts which they entirely fail to catch; and is not that exactly the way in which men of mere intellect, or rather, mere first-Adamic men move among second-Adamic men? They are among them, but not of them. This is true whether the men in question be virtuous or not. If, however, they are virtuous, and come up to the first-Adamic make by having good consciences, then they appreciate and love Christians, and are, many of them, not far from the Kingdom; but still they regard Christians with a kind of wonder, and think they go too far. The fact is, the latter are "*new*" men and women, while those who are fashioned after the former type and who are not born again, but who have the comfort of being lovely and pleasant in their lives, often are content with the attainments of that grade of being, and do not care to be risen with Christ. But in some parts of the planet the air is so full of spores of the Christ-nature, and so many seeds of divine words fly about, that such honest and good hearts as these are very likely to be dusted with the *farina* of the new life, and then they arise, and their eyes are opened, and they have joy unspeakable and full of glory.

184.

ALL that I have, without myself,
Is not enough for Thee ;
Without Thyself, not all Thou hast
Can be enough for me.

185.

Isa. lxi. 3.

BEYOND doubt the climate of celestial immortality, that glorious conservatory of the blest, will bring forth in the lives of many of our kinsfolk and acquaintance blooms of grace which now the most far-seeing among us would laugh outright at the thought of. May we be there to see, and to be, the subjects of this shouting merriment of the sons of God.

186.

THERE are three sisters, who are called Grace, Mercy, and Peace. What pleasant names to be always sounding through a household.

187.

"BLESSED are they that have not seen and yet have believed." This seems to mean also, Blessed are they who have not seen with the mental eye *how* things are, but who yet know with their hearts that what Christ tells them is truth ; whose hearts grasp the Saviour's ὅτι, though their minds fail to see His διότι ; who are too delicate to press Him further when He says, "What I do thou knowest not now, but thou shalt know hereafter," but who do not on that account, in vulgar dudgeon, "go away, and walk no more with Him."

I know in WHOM,— *S. Paul.*

188.

WHEN the divine light breaks on our landscape, what was dark becomes illumined, and outlines of unimagined charm spring forth from shadows which before seemed one massive neutrality.

189.

IT is only by my fault that I am not better than I am ; only by Thy mercy that I am not worse than I am.

Isa. xxvi. 12.

Ne quid nimis.

190.

THE unwise and wholesale maintenance of principles is like to go far to ruin the world. The principle of religious toleration is giving full swing to the power of Rome on the one hand, and to State-irreligion on the other. Rome, being free from the State, has the whip-hand of a Church which is yoked with it, and she can do almost as much good or harm as she likes. Meet is it changes should control our national being. "God fulfils Himself in many ways, lest one good custom should corrupt the world." The best part of the world is becoming corrupted by indiscriminate toleration. It is a watchword dealt in over much. May Providence fulfil Himself in the modification of this good custom. It is but a burlesque of Freedom. Freedom itself is a golden mean. The sense of this in the nation is at the bottom of the late reaction in favour of Conservatism. So far, at least, may God speed it.

ὥστε τῷ
καπνῷ
πάντας
Ἕλληνας
δακρῦσαι.
Aristoph.

191.

Corruptio optimi est pessimum. By implication, *Perfectio pessimi fit optimum.*

192.

WHAT if the end of the world were to come down upon us instead of our ending during its progress ? What if our Sun were to suffer a sky-change, such as we saw a kindred Sun suffer but yesterday ? If we had an hour's warning, how easy we should feel during that hour about the persons who would not then be left behind, or about the works half done, which we might not have had time to finish and which would not then need finishing. All those feelings which any of us may have of desire to be remem- bered ; of leaving, at least among our countrymen or friends, if not for world- wide use, thoughts and emotions by which our memory may be endeared, and by which being dead we still may speak :—all these things would then cease to move us. Papers would want no arranging ; no mementoes would want leaving, no messages sending ; no disagreeable anticipations would haunt us, or flit before us, of being laid out and wept for ; we should be on the alert for flight ; ready to be carried off from the ruins of the world ; looking on the tip-toe of

For who to dull forget- fulness a prey — ?
Gray.

εἰ γὰρ
μετακύ-
μιος ἄτας,
ὦ Παιὰν,
φανείης.
Soph.

expectation for the coming of the Son of Man. We should leave our houses and walk abroad, and watch the heavens ; and, if real and humble believers, I think we should lift up our heart and voice, and sing aloud for our Redemption drawing nigh. And yet, if all our little affairs are now in clear order, arranged for death ; if we are working while it is day ; if we are trusting our unfinished works, as well we may, constantly in the Master's hands ; if we leave with calm common-sense the accidents of our dissolution to be got over by our Christian kindred in the course of nature—why, thus we may contemplate the end of this life, come when or how it may, with much the same good-humour as if we knew we had but another hour on the planet, and may say always, "Come, Lord Jesus, come quickly." And yet this is the only condition in which those should be living, who are in the habit of travelling on lines dependent on the overwrought nerves of one signalman.

Uncertainty in a danger-signal is certainly a signal danger.

193.

As you advance you seem to be getting more and more alone into your speciality of capacity, your special modes of doing your part on earth, and your special facilities of accepting the advices of Heaven. This being so, you will feel that, but for God, you would be left more and more lonely in life. But as your Christ becomes more and more revealed in you, and as He reveals to you more and more your hope of your special glory, you feel less and less alone, because the Father is with you. You may well pray as you look forward, " If Thy presence go *not* with me, carry me not up hence." To grow, but not to grow in Christ, is a desolate prospect indeed.

> And yet I am nct alone, because the Father is with me.
> CHRIST.

194.

As in the moral life feelings are to principles, so, in the intellectual, cleverness is to the power of logical inference. The same natures usually have the corresponding terms of this proportion. In which sex you commonly find which terms, it would be invidious to enquire. You may often find in a mind a delicacy of observation, a brilliancy of repartee, a rapidity of application, and a wide range of ideas, with an unusual facility of association, and you may be strongly impressed with an opinion of great ability: but once come to close quarters in a discussion where your truth has to fight its way inch by inch through phalanxes of fallacies and to storm successive outworks of objection, it is marvellous how quickly all these high powers can collapse, and how all that shining array of imposing abilities will troop off discomfited and prove itself phantasmal. Educators will find it well, after having practised the memory mainly till the age of eleven, as I remember once to have heard Dr. Arnold remark, to practise thenceforth also the powers of practical ratiocination. This should be done, not principally in necessary truth, for life has very little to do with such truth, except in some of the sciences ; but in contingent matter, that is to say, in the matter of human life. To this practice of reasoning those lighter powers should be made to minister.

195.

HER talk was neither large nor small ;
Of neither mind nor mirth was lack;
How gracefully she caught my ball,
And toyed with it, and tossed it back !

'Twas pleasant to behold the play,
The flashing merciless intent,
Wherewith, before she stood at bay,
She spent her light-armed argument.

Self-gathered now she quick prepares
Her massed, her main defence—but lo !
Scattered are all her pretty squares
Before my cry of " divido."

And yet, such honour fired her van,
When all her fairy lines were broke,
In winning ways, as women can,
Her cruel losses out she spoke.

I could not find the heart to beat,
And gladly strained a point to find
A way to cover the retreat
Of such a gallant little mind.

And though, for very Truth's dear sake,
I dared not let her win that day,
I gave her—what she would not take ;—
The conquered man I moved away !

196.

THERE are still nebulous and floating masses of humanity, Tartars, Sclaves, African tribes and the like, out of which our Creator is gradually shaping civil societies. From these, in due time, nations may form themselves, that will orb about in the Family-system of States. Perhaps, as they grow into an orderly sense of right, they will be warned by our recorded errors, and will develop the fruits of Christian life better than our older nations, which have so long been revolving in the sunshine of knowledge and are yet so barren. Yet what they *will be* depends in dreadful proportion on what *we are*. If we eliminate the Christ-nature from our States, we, *pejores avis, daturi sumus progeniem vitiosiorem.*

197.

WHAT is charity itself but the elevation and refinement of fairness ? Have perfect the one virtue of fairness, and you will have all virtues perfect. So indeed with each of the virtues all round, a *dictum* of Aristotle which will bear the closest investigation.

198.

NOTE the extraordinary accuracy with which St. John gives the account of the endeavours made by the Jews to overthrow the miracle of the opening of the eyes of the man who had been born blind. The same also may be said of the account of the raising of Lazarus. They doubtless took great, if not equal, pains to overthrow many more, if not most of the great miracles. These accounts seem given us as samples. The Master of Trinity, in a lecture on the Phædrus of Plato, told us he did not at the moment remember a better instance of that ἀγροῖκος σοφία—that wisdom of clowns which Socrates turns to scorn with lips half divine—than the explanation of the miracles of the loaves and fishes given by that German Professor, who said that the multitude brought food in their pockets !

βλέπον-
τες ἔβλεπ-
ον μάτην.
Æsch.

199.

FACIES non omnibus una
Nec diversa tamen, qualem decet esse sororum.
Ovid.
Not all the selfsame lines of face had caught,
Yet, if they varied, 'twas as sisters ought.

200.

IN how many persons you do not see—I had rather say in how few you do see—the full beauty of their character and the full play of their nature. This is especially so in the case of those lower natures who have not yet admitted the working of the Spirit of Christ ; but it holds true of Christians also. They rarely fulfil their Master's joy. But kindly remember how much this is due to their surroundings. Plant them in happy circumstances, where they shall be attended by love and encompassed by sympathy, and you will soon see what exquisite flowers, hitherto unsuspected, will be called forth and will start up in their lives. Then, if never before, will they show themselves free bloomers.

Tibi suaveis dædala tellus Summittit flores. *Lucr.*

Rev. iv. 1.

201.

THE firs that feather black on the blue—
  That is an English wood ;
Yon sea-line faint that bounds my view—
  That is our English flood ;
The scent of the May from the whitened vale as
  far as mine eye can tell—
It makes me love my life the more, that this is
  an English smell.

202.

WHEN you wake in the morning, the more or less rapid return of consciousness is on this wise : (1) "I am ;" (2) "I am myself;" (3) "I am here." So, when a man awakes and Christ gives him light, he finds (1) that he is ; then for the first time he realises his true being. (2) He finds that he is special, the result of antecedents and a unique combination of powers. The true way in which to fulfil his being is one of which nobody else can exactly judge. Having found "Such am I," (3) he asks, "Where am I ? " Then he finds himself in a certain time and age, with a certain personal *entourage* in relationships near or far, and in a place that has its own needs. He is amidst channels for his influence, and means of living out that new life :—in which thus the first step was the cognition of it ; the second, the cognition of his own character ; the third, the recognition of his proper sphere. Then, and not till then, he is broad awake.

Awake and sing, ye that dwell in the dust.
THE SPIRIT OF GOD.

203.

IT is, I suppose, in little things that self-control is most difficult to acquire and most heartily to be admired. We reverence a man who to one that insolently attacks him in a public assembly answers by a wise smile and a meek reply. We reverence him, I say, profoundly ; and he also has his outward reward in the collaudation of a sympathising audience. But he does not, I confess, challenge so large a share of my admiration as the man who, being naturally of an irritable disposition, in the perfect solitude of his own dressing-room, can, without one stamp of his foot, one cloud upon his brow, one twitch of his lip, find himself, when dinner is waiting for him, without a button on the collar of his shirt.

Hæc via sola fuit quâ perdere posses. *Verg.*

204.

A LAW of gravitation prevails in Spiritual things, and perhaps under God a higher form of it orders our eternal future. The co-operation of this with Will and Love prevents the concourse of causes from being fortuitous.

205.

How pleasant and hopeful it is, if ever we find a change for the better. Take a man whom we knew to be base, or at least believed to be so, or whom we thought ill-tempered, crabbed or disagreeable. Some remedial plant has re-arranged some functional working; some change in fortune has sweetly come down upon him from the Father of all good; perhaps more often than anything it is that he has lit upon love. One or other of these things causes all that which we thought to be inherent in him and a part of the man, to vanish like some noxious vapour dissipated by the breathing of the sweet south. How blessed, how hopeful this is; how charitable it should make us in our estimates one of another; how anxious by all means that may lie in our special power to cause the Sun of prosperity to shine upon our fellows. That was not an evil little girl who said, "I wish unhappiness would not make me feel naughty." Well may the observation of such change in others lead us to hope that in our own case, at least in the resurrection,

Bless me, even me also, oh my Father.

if not before, the sins and weaknesses against which here we have to struggle, may vanish into the thin airs of that immortal region in which we hope to God we may use the oarage of new wings.

206.

THE Star of Morning pours his beam
Upon the wild and wayward rill;
And when it flows a deeper stream,
The same sweet Star stands o'er it still.

207.

THE signs of water, bread, and wine, are connecting links between spirit and matter, authorised by Jesus.

208.

Drunk delight of battle. *Tenn.*

YOU should learn to love most to do the right things which you like least, and to find a high delight in going clean against your lower grain.

209.

If the foundations be destroyed—? Ps. xi. 3.

DO not let your will be weak, nor let the function of resolution be ignored in anything, however slight ; for thus the speck of corruption lights on the principle of action.

210.

THE Sea in long, strong, deep-furrowed, successive sweeps, careering against Old England, that holds it long in mastery, comes milk-white against her, and tosses to the sky crests discoloured with her soil, which soil *never can be recovered.* Thus "ocean sweeps the laboured mole away " wherever groynes are not wisely made, and beetling cliffs are sapped till they fall, never again to be part of this country. Whole parishes along the South and the East coast have disappeared, almost within the memory of man. Stones of their old churches are said to be visible at low water. But coast-lines, which for each generation are the property of individuals, seem in fact also the property of all the generations which from first to last hold England from the Landlord of the planet; and so they ought perhaps to be the care of all ongoing Governments. Yet, for want of power, it is said, to grapple with the complex question of tenure, England is throwing her fairest edges into the sea. Pray look to this, ye wise statesmen. Ye are treating our ma-

ΩΚ.
παραιν-
έσαι γέ
σοι θέλω
τὰ λῷστα·
Γίγνωσκε
σαυτὸν
καὶ μεθάρ-
μοσαι
τρόπους
νέους.
Æsch.

terial mother as badly as some of you would treat the State-Christianity, "which is the Mother of us all." Here too it is the complexity of tenure which is the puzzle. But that you must get over as best you may. My neighbour, who can tell the signs of the Sea, says, "What matters? You can't check the changes of the planet. Let England go when she becomes too dear to keep. When the islands of Wales and Westmoreland become too small for you, go somewhere else." Well, this may be so. England's greatness rests, I know, not on *where* she is, but on *what* she is. Woe be to her indeed, if she "sets the how much before the how." And this is why I implore Statesmen to take heed lest that better country, that is the heavenly, be lost and vanish from our midst, or leave but a few wretched ruins on the sands of a barren past.

211.

IF you first come to know in *Whom* to believe, you will soon come to know in *what* to believe.

212.

Except our hearts be pure, guileless, contented, and beholding the face of the unseen Eternal Father, we cannot bear well
either a grief or a joy.   We sail in a drizz-
ling fog.   So it is good that we pray thus:
" Heavenly Father, clear off from my soul
all clouds, that I may see Thee as Thou
art, and that so I may bear well all that
comes from Thee."

γέγηθε δέ
τε φρένα
ποιμήν.
Hom.

213.

WHAT becomes of forgotten ideas ?   Do
they insensibly fall into the ground of the
mind, and, like last year's leaves, enrich it
for future produce ?

οὐδέν ἢ
φύσις
μάτην
ποιεῖ.
Arist.

*   *   *   *

O let us look on each cold thought
As we shall look upon it *then*—
When one, whose love we set at nought,
Has gone—and will not come again.

214.

TO preach, you must teach; to teach, you
must touch; and to touch, you must be
touched by that live coal which God lays
on the lips of His messengers.

215.

FATHER, be by me when I come to die;
Deal thou with me as I was wont of yore
To deal with yon toy-craft, that heedfully
I sent forth-faring from the firm-set shore:
When I am launching on thine Evermore,
Come to that verge of Immortality;
Fix me fair linen, ample, aft and fore,
Secure its threadage lest it flap and fly;
My rudder fast at some just angle set
To catch what breezes are careering by;
These temper, for Thou canst, lest billow-beat
I founder in yon vast Infinity:
But most I pray Thee, ever hold in hand
A line—to draw me somewhere safe to land.

216.

I SAW a battle to-day : the storming of a
citadel. The citadel was Bognor, and the
storming was—by the storm. The pleasure-
walk was the glacis. It was happily a
weather-tide, for the wind blew W.N.W.
The siege-train was set in motion about
eleven o'clock. The Queen commanded
in person, and had taken up her position
on an eminence 30,000 miles nearer than
she usually does when leading these forces
against these defences. We stood outside
the range of smoke, shingle, and shell; and
watched what passed. The whole plain up
to the horizon was a moving series of for-
lorn hopes, armed as in mottled plate and
scale armour, which fitted so well that it
seemed in the light and shade to suit itself
to the least play of the body, as the troops
came up under the sway of the undulation of
onset. They advanced in terrible sternness ;
and if the line wavered or showed any irregularity, it was not from any looseness of
order, but from the quivering of great
strength in rapid motion, and from very
firmness of stroke, as when an artist draws

a line. While these kept up running dis-
charges, the clouds of smoke feathered off
to the South East, hiding the sky half-way
up to the zenith, and lifting lacey veils
against the sun. Then, and then only,
could we catch the flash and play of the
colours, as they rose and sank in the confused noise of the charge. I never saw
Byron's images of "love watching madness,"
and "hope on a death-bed," set forth so
beautifully, since I saw them at Terni.
There indeed they wore " unalterable
mien " : here they were but fitful.

By 1.30 all was done that could be done
that day ; and Bognor still stands, kept up
by us poor Ratepayers for the pleasure of
those who in the summer will come to see
the smiling battle-fields of winter. The
lovers of grandeur should come while they
can, and visit us what time the storms fall
upon us.

217.

THOSE that love the Lord never meet for
" the last time."

218.

How important it is to the life of the
mind, nay of the spiritual life, to keep your
independence.   Keep the mean between
being too little like your neighbours and
too much like them.   This is a rule for
politics, social converse, Theology, and for all
morals.   Be careful not to get swamped, and
do not let your individuality become merged
and lost in other people's ways of thinking.
And in this age of books, take heed how ye
read.   Do not let your mental conscience
be troubled and clouded by feeling always,
" *This* must necessarily be read, and *that* is
essential to full knowledge, and nothing
can be known well without so-and-so."   It
may be so, but discriminate wisely in this.
Remember that you have your own life,
your special powers, special aims, and special sphere to cherish and preserve.   And in
like manner be not either too closely wed-
ded to, or too lightly divorced from your
own "manner of spirit."   While you bring for
your food and for your teaching, if you have
to teach, old things out of your treasures of
records or of memory, take heed also to have

γνῶθι
σ'αὐτον.

a permanent and living treasure *within your-self*, out of which you may ever be able to bring new things. Harvest and garner well what you gather either from your reading, or study, or reflection. If you guard these rules, you will find "new lights will ever round you rise." "The trivial round, the common task," and kindly but wise observation, will supply you with ideas new to yourself, and pleasant and profitable to those with whom you mix, and from whom, if your *entourage* be of kindred spirit, you may always keep learning, while you for your part minister what you may. But keep *your own* spirit, your own mind, your own heart diligently, for out of them are the issues of your own personal life, which to you is of more importance than that of anybody else ever can be.

219.

The Milken Way.

THE Earth under Heaven is lain,
  At the fount of her life and her rest;
And yon is a branching vein
  Streaking that bountiful breast.

220.

A REASON against monotone seems to be that it is apt to ignore the Personal Element in the Universe and to deny that God is a Person in whose image we are. Nobody would earnestly speak with a Person in that way. You might speak with an impersonal fetish in that uninterested tone upon a kind of understanding with the fetish in yourself, that it was no matter; but no one whose words were expressing their thoughts and feelings, would in the first instance, and till taught by habit, plead and pray in this way with a living Person, of whom they believed themselves to be the suffering children. In fact monotone seems to me to be, originally at least, a device of Ritualism to swamp genuine humanity in the worshippers, and to give an impression that spirit and truth are irrelevant and not to be expected in or from humanity. I am far from saying it is always so now; any persons, even the good, earnest, and holy, may become accustomed to any mode; but in its beginning this was not natural. It exactly suits with the form of godliness without the

ἄπτερος
ἔπλετο
μῦθος.
Hom.

power. And if monotone is really found to be the only audible mode of prayer in Cathedrals or large Churches, then what I say falls to the ground in those cases. It is not to the singing that I object, for to those to whom singing is natural—that is, to most people—to pray thus is natural and agreeable and highly suitable to some states of the soul; but inflexible or unflexed monotone I cannot away with. Some people are wont to read poetry in too high and unearthly a tone, but it merges the meaning, and sends us to sleep. Not but what, both in prayers and in reciting good poetry, the tone, as in eloquence, will naturally assume a certain rapt elevation.

221.

Vicinitas, quod ego in propinquâ parte amicitiæ puto.
   Ter.

WHEN a man finds that he and his neighbours cannot "get on," it is usually his own fault. In which case the best thing for his neighbours, and for himself also, is that, as soon as possible, he "get off." But usually he is the last to see this, and is rather disposed to use the lauguage of the hedgepig.

222.

I DOUBT if a man of bad life can freely, thoroughly, and thoughtfully enjoy the company even of a dog. His debased and corrupted nature feels ill at ease beside the orderly, unspoiled instinct of the beast. He is conscious, if he reflects, of a super-incumbent weight of disordered capacities and an infinite stratum of twisted inactivities. Even if he be not pained by the reflection, still this is true, and the mere fact must weigh upon his life. The dog is a natural and respectable being, and is doubtless uncomfortable beside him. The dog knows when his companion is not genuine, even when the man's dissatisfaction with himself does not, like Grandcourt's, break out into ill-temper.

συντρά-
πεζος.
Batr.

νὴ τὸν
κύνα.
Socrates.

223.

THERE cannot be a better proof of a prop than this : that we find it bears our weight. We bear up best when we lean on God most. He surely lives Whom we cannot live without, and, having Whom most, we find that we live best.

Αἴτιος
τοῦ εἶναι,
ὄντος
μεγίστου.
Arist.

224.

SHALL we say that, because the Gospel according to St. John differs in tone from that of the others, that therefore it does not give a correct photograph of the thoughts and sayings of Christ? Is it very unreasonable to suppose that, of the many sides of Christ, there was one side which none could catch and reflect, or which at least none caught and reflected, but John? Do we not know men who, without duplicity or irony, unfold themselves differently to different friends, and who have aspects of their mind on which only those who are especially gifted that way are at liberty to look? Do not whole conversations pass from some minds, all of which have impressed themselves on the minds of others? Have we not often talked with those who have brought out from us, or from whom we have brought out, ranges of consciousness which had been dormant till then, and which but for that occasion would never have been awakened at all? What if Christ had said some of those many other things which he had to say? And he *would* have said them,

had he found any one able to bear them.
We should have had more battles about
authenticity and genuineness; for those
things would have been found to be unlike
anything which He said to others, who
could bear other things, but not those.

*νηλεῶς
ὧδ' ἐρρύθ-
μισμαι.
Æsch.*

225.

I ONCE heard one say, in a queer, melancholy mood, "I should like to find somewhere somebody else's cast-off happiness"
—as if it would have fitted! Goldsmith
instructs thee very well, thus saying:

"Vain, very vain, thy weary search to find
That happiness which centres in the mind."

226.

WHEN a man is unwell, his work is to
rest: when well, his best rest often is to
work, but in both cases in due measure and
with wise variety. When a man is "pur-
bled up," as they say in Lincolnshire, with
necessary but uncongenial business, his
hardest work is not to be able to *get at* his
work.

*Pendent
opera in-
terrupta.
V.*

227.

Is the spirit of martyrdom so very rare?
Do we not know many who would rather
die than distinctly break one of God's ac-
knowledged commandments? Indeed do
we know any respectable person who would
not die rather than lose his character by
infringing certain parts of the moral law?
Nay, if it comes to being ready to die,
people we know will die, by the dozens, for
very brief and very questionable gains.
Some ladies consciously incur death in order,
for the few short and painful years which
they allot to themselves, to cultivate waists
like insects. Some will do so in order to
keep some one habit, as the habit of lifting
the little finger in the air and stinging the
roof of the mouth. The braying of an ass
has always struck me as expressive of the
agonies of a martyr in some bad or foolish
cause. The world is full of such martyrs,
and yet fools count those to be fanatical,
who die with their Master because they regard Life as more than meat!

οὐ γὰρ
ἔστι τἀμ-
φανῆ
κρύπτειν.
Soph.

228.

By idle persons, or persons in part or sometimes idle, one duty often does not get tackled with, or at least properly grappled with, till the time has arrived for the doing of another. Duties are not kept pace with duly, and so they tumble over each others' heels. This vice especially befalls the unpractical, the deep-contemplative, the unwisely speculative, some who are late in the morning and late at night, and the dreamy. It overcomes the kind of spirit which is apt to languish and hanker after what it has not, or what it thinks it might have been, instead of vigourously and rigourously making the best of what it has and is, and doing τὰ πρὸς ποσί—*anglicè*, the things before the nose.

μυρίων
ἐπιστρο-
φαὶ κακῶν
Soph.

229.

It is astonishing what numbers of people saddle Balaam's speaking ass with their religious difficulty; certainly they are the very last who should express a marvel on that head.

De te narra-
tur. *Hor.*

230.

To revive yourself, think of the prophets and Psalmists and of CHRIST, and of the blest of all times, and the good whom you know and love ; and then you will surely be ashamed, for any passing pleasure, much more for mere sloth, to fall away from their glorious company, and to desert from that noble Army.

The loss of shame is every sin in one.
William Mallock.

231.

WEALTH hardly gotten spend not over-lightly,
And what flows freely dam not up too tightly.

232.

OUR bodies at first were sprinkled three times with water. They will at last be sprinkled three times with dust. What of τὰ μεταξύ τούτων ? oh momentous interval ! Oh " traveller between life and death," thou mayst well "breathe thoughtful breath."

In the name of the Father, and of the Son, and of the Holy Ghost.

Earth to earth, ashes to ashes, dust to dust.

233.

THE proof of the Bread of Life is in its eating.

234.

IN reading Wesley's hymns we must remember as to some of those utterances of prevailing weakness, that he probably made them not so much for himself as for the use of new converts and for the people in general. Readers should always be on their guard against the temptation to localise and crystallise with unfair personality the expressions of authors, especially of preachers; and more especially of poets, whose imagination, by its very function, glancing from heaven to earth, from earth to heaven, bodies forth the forms of things unseen, and things which need not have the remotest reference to their own personal history.

Prenez, Madame J., prenez de meilleures lunettes. *Moliere.*

235.

IN expressing a hope of prosperity, you mean "a revival of business." Yes, but then remember, there is no business so momentous as your *soul's* business,—that your *soul* should prosper. No revival of your business is so important as this business of your "revival."

τῇ φακῇ μύρον.

Our fortune lies upon this jump. *Shaks.*

K

236.

BY pressing a matter unduly a man may sometimes so break up a Council or a Board upon a detail or upon a mode, as to produce the appearance of difference, where in fact there is a grounded agreement—whereby he gratuitously defeats his main purpose. He is the wiser President or Chairman, who can find, through agreement upon details or upon matters of secondary importance, modes of prolonging the chances of ultimate concord.

Consilium vultu tegit. V.

237.

IF Heaven has placed thee labour's need above,
'Tis wholesome still to labour—but for love.

238.

Jam certus eundi. V.

IT is an excellent thing for a man to know to whom to run for safety, should he find himself attacked by mental, mental-moral, or by physical or physico-moral dangers. Except he knows something about Christ, or how to get to Him, he is indeed in a serious dilemma, and comes to a dead standstill, or falls. Lord, to whom shall we go? Thou only hast the words of Eternal Life.

239.

THE love of God is quite as much a *principle* as a feeling. It must be *both* to be perfect, for principle stands as the body to the spirit of feeling ; but at any rate it must be a principle, or else it cannot be known to live. Show me a man who performs some duty, or abstains from some besetting sin, under the glow and impulse of some stirring and fervid emotion, and I will love and honour him, and thank God for his noble act, or still nobler self-denial ; nay, I will hope for him that successive acts, and successive self-denials of the like kind may form in him some day a safe and steady habit of allegiance. But, on the other hand, show me a man who has no such strong and pleasant feeling to blow in his sail ; who knows no such delightful frame to comfort and reward him ; whose feelings, alas for the weakness of the flesh, set quite the other way, and counteract the willingness of his spirit ; whose frame, perhaps from circumstances which he cannot at once control, is of a contrary humour :—find me, I say, such a man, who yet—as a matter of course, as a matter of principle, as a matter of duty, rule, and law—goes through a course of right action against wind and stream, with his face towards the better world—and I will tell you, judging from the facts of character, whether of the twain is the more likely to reach the port. Whatever hopes we may have for the former, this latter is, in all reason, the more likely, from his constant and steady adherence to a rule and law of life, to acquire by practice the ease and pleasure of the perfect habit; a pleasure which will be, not the hectic flush of the soul's excitement, but the regular glow of its daily and hourly health.

In years (s)he seemed, but not impaired by years. *Pope.*

And herein, methinks, it is that the Church, to which there still adheres the pleasant name of England, more especially promises to be the saving of our Country's religion. It is not without meaning that the nation allows its great name still to cling to its ancient forms of Faith. It is not without reason that our Queen retains her place at the head of our national Church. When the masses of the people, who in the first burst of their freedom are disporting themselves somewhat wildly away from the fold of their ancestral shelter, have become still more severed and scattered by the worrying of their ill-trained collies, and by the disintegration which must accompany excitement—then, when the hour of Providence shall have come, it will be seen how grandly this our Church of England, except before then she be spoiled by her own priests, will come upon these decomposed masses ; affectionately gather back, as she now longs to do, the wandering flocks into her fold of souls ; and herself rise up into a fairer and surer inheritance. Oh what a Church will be there !

I was led naturally into this track of thought when dwelling on the love of God being not a mere feeling, but a principle also. But what if there shall be no longer a State-Church left to do this ? The programme which I have pictured for her will be swept off, if the prestige of her position shall be gone. Her very name will have first to go ! What business will she have to keep any longer the name of England, when the authority and paternity of England is gone

Quem vocet Divum popu!us ruentis Imperi rebus?
Hor.

δάπτει δὲ
καὶ τὸ
μὴ ἔνδικ-
ον.
Soph.

from her? She will be legally bastardised. What other name will they be able to find for her? Her enemies—nay her friends, so far as they can be distinguished from her enemies, will hardly find any other name for her than that of Rome. She will say "I will go to my house from whence I came out." In this respect at least—I do not say in any other—her pale ghost will be like that which goes about seeking rest, and she will find none but on the Seven Hills. As for the prayer-book of the new sect, the Queen, by way of compliment, may be called "gracious," but to call the Majesty of England —then a "buried Majesty"—"most religious," would be a gross impertinence. So far as Her Rule is concerned, She will have become our Pay-mistress and our Executioner, and no more!

Sera in
cœlum
redeas, diu-
que læta in-
tersis.
Hor.

You do it
wrong, being
so majes-
tical, to offer
it the show
of violence.
Shaks.

240.

Lacteolæ
animæ.
Lucr.

RITES are the bottles in which the milk of the Divine life is raised to the lips of the soul. Souls are nourished by rites precisely as much as babes by bottles.

241.

DOES any man pretend to run down a good "frame," as they call it, or a good feeling? Oh friend, if thou hast any of these to spare, tell me where thou walkest, and if thou throwest any away, I will follow thee and pick them up behind thee how thankfully! If he means the same thing as I do, he cannot be in his senses, if he would discard so inestimable a blessing as a good frame. The presence of a good frame is more by far than the presence of health; and the absence of joyous feeling is the very headache and heartache of the soul. Without these good frames and feelings how are we, as St. Paul bids us, to "rejoice evermore"? And commonly, though not always and necessarily, a good frame encloses a good picture. It is difficult to see how principles themselves can flourish in any other air than that of these "frames and feelings" of which we speak. Of that spiritual drunkenness of vulgar fanaticism, that semi-slavish buffoonery, into which, even on this side the Atlantic, Faith seems to be running to seed under the large and

Dulcia non meruit qui non gustavit amara.
Old tomb in Chichester Cathedral

Damnosa hereditas.

much-abused name of "Methodism,"—I have nothing to say here.

242.

O BLESSED, oh cursed ink !—as air of loquend, so thou art the life-blood or death-blood of scribend thoughts !

[Let gerundive forms be pardoned when they are convenient. *" Cur ego invideor "* ? If our mother tongue has not the word which we want for expressing our idea, there is nothing left for us but to coin one for our purpose. No one need adopt it, who does not want to do so.]

Linque sev-
era. *Hor.*

We grant
thou canst
outscold us.
Shaks.

243.

You cannot help it now—look not so sad—
Such sorrow cannot better what was bad.

244.

I KNOW of nothing more important than this :—that you should reserve to yourself the power, by God's grace, of breaking short off all bad habits, whether physical, mental, or moral, so soon as ever they begin to creep over you in a succession of single acts.

τὶς γαρ
ἐσθλὸς
οὐχ αὐτῷ
φίλος ;

245.

I SELDOM watch a ship coming into the harbour-mouth, but that I think of one of the souls of the blest entering the "place prepared" for it. And, just as in persons that stand about a death-bed, so there is mostly an interest created by the vessel's entrance, even if it be but a cutter or a coal-brig ; some kindly concern, not merely in the minds of the owner and his servants, but among the common folk grouped on the quay. Aye, and if the usual appliances, the tug or the horses, be not at hand or be occupied elsewhere, it seldom fails but that a company of such stalwart men as the pier affords spring forward without waiting for a challenge, to lift her in, lest she should lose the tide and so be thrown back again on the perilous neighbourhood of the shore. And those who may be appointed to help in such cases seldom charge with irregularity those who offer their help freely.

246.

It will not ruin *thee* this sum to lack,
Which it would ruin *him* to pay thee back.

Transform me to what shape Thou wilt, I pass not what it be.

Drayton.

247.

WHAT an airy-light thing is this spirit of man! The houses abide that he built, the trees flourish that he planted—even the little deciduous shrubs keep coming out in their appointed season ; but the generations of the spirits of men, coming also from the Unseen, leave those solid blocks and long-lived vegetables, step how lightly back again to the bosom of God, and we see them no more—as yet. Passing unseen through the crowd of seen concerns, and the shut doors of matter, they hope to find themselves in some Upper Chamber of the New Jerusalem, at the prepared Table in the prepared place, eating bread in the kingdom of God, and to hear from "the Father Himself"—"Joy be unto you."

248.

ἔρρει τὰ θεῖα.

Soph.

WELL-INTENTIONED men often do as much harm as ill-intentioned ; just as we find foolish travellers do as much harm by chipping sacred spots out of love, as irreligious men do, that hack them out of hatred.

249.

IF you have never tried, you do not *know* what a high interest always attaches to working out your own state of Salvation in Christ. You will really find it worth trying. Go to some discreet and learned Christian, who knows in Whom he has believed, and he will tell you all about it, and put you on the right tack. If you are not singular, you take an interest in your body and its dress, in your mind and its culture. Why should you not take an interest in your *soul?* Surely it is *very* eccentric not to do so.

Incipe, parve puer, cognoscere— V.

250.

THE good traits which we thankfully note in a character may either be the first of a dawn, the lights of ongoing day, or the last of a sunset. In like manner, the bad traits we note may either be the first of the incoming night, or part of the deepening night, or the last of the off-going night. He who "knows what is in man" alone can judge. "Judge not that ye be not judged ; Condemn not, that ye be not condemned."

251.

TAKE a bad man in suffering, and then take a good :—one growls and groans beneath his distresses, or at best takes them as things that must be endured. The Christian has a joy hidden beneath them, as compared with which the merriest moments of the worldling are hollow melancholy, the laugh of the maniac contrasted with the calm satisfaction of a man in his right mind. Which is the more philosophical—this, or "to grin and bear it"? Yet the latter is the "dernier ressort" of your philosopher! If the poor rogue *can't* grin, there is nothing left for him—but chagrin.

Then to the tub again, for a new pickle. Beau. & F.

252.

IT is a very dangerous thing for the eye to dwell with pleasure on loveable forms to which a man is not in the position to stand honestly related. Vague desires arise which create at least discomfort and unsettlement. Set purposes and steady aims, waver, and the key of the nature becomes lowered; and this perhaps without any thought of sin.

The giddy pleasure of the eyes. Tenn.

253.

How inhuman is mere hard, bright mind! How metallic in its ring! It seems so un-get-at-able; so perfect in the joints of its logical harness, so unanswerable, so complete, leaving nothing more to be said —and yet, *subter-human*. It is like a wintry ground. The atmosphere is clear and all is clean and white; but there is no greenness, no growth, nothing genial and warm, kind and considerate. From having, or from clashing with *mere* hard, bright intellect, good Lord deliver us! Ten times rather give us an honest stupidity.

Those frosts
which winter
brings,
Which candy
every green.
Drayton.

254.

As man is made up of spirit and matter, so truth is combined of chastened imagination and accurate fact. A bare fact is often a barefaced falsehood. Imagination, when in the air, is a "delusive faculty." But when fact and imagination, that is, an exact conception of the circumstances, check and limit each other, then in all honesty and wisdom you arrive at clear and wholesome truth.

ἆρ' ἔστιν,
ἆρ' οὐκ
ἔστιν;
Soph.

255.

"THE king of Ashantee consults his Fetishes, and their omens give adverse answers." It is odd that the human mind in its degraded condition should firmly believe in the false power, and yet that civilised people should not so firmly believe in the real Power, Whose existence alone can account for the phantasy of such a power in the object of superstition. If I see the sun reflected in a duck-pond, however filthy be the reflection, it is no less a sign of the sun.

256.

CHRIST did not turn the water into His wine till all the common wine was done. So men's evil nature was not to be made better by Christ's goodness: but Christ's goodness was to come and occupy and renew our hearts. Our Salvation was not to be a mixed concern.

"Give me to drink."

257.

EVERYTHING seems unsafe without knowledge.

Omnia tuta timens. *v.*

258.

A SUFFICIENT reason for maintaining the distinctness between spirit and matter is this. If you regard them as jumbled up on even terms, then unseen law, which must be recognised by all as a delicate power, is dragged down and imbruted. Their union throughout Nature is set forth in the highest range by the marriage betwixt Christ and His Church.

Like perfect music unto noble words.
Tenn.

259.

A MAN who is a physician to himself— and therefore not in that respect a fool— avoids certain articles of food, which, however pleasant, he finds to disagree with him. So also will it be with the person who is a moral physician to himself.

Annis gravis atque animi maturus.
V.

260.

"THY will be done, as in heaven, so on earth" means, among other things, "Thy will be done, as in our spiritual nature, so in our dust and in our lower desires ; may our earthly desires be in accordance with Thy heavenly nature within us."

261.

SUPPOSE, if possible, Christ not to be what He says He is—what becomes of the aspirations, the lives, the spirits of St. Paul, Thomas à Kempis, Legh Richmond, Charles Bridges, Keble, Arnold, and of the good, afflicted poor to whom any minister can point among his people? They would be vain! Now can anything be so unphilosophical as to set these sane men down as vain men, because some professors of this or that physical science have lost, or have never yet found the faculties to understand their hopes? These leaders, not of thought but of lower observation, can observe signs in earth, or sky, or sea, or anywhere else; but not the sign of the Son of God in their own spirit! Therefore *of course* they cannot read it in the spirit of any one else. But is that high philosophy? It is truly an *insipiens sapientia,* only valuable so far as it goes.

" Let the cobbler stick to his last."

262.

" ETERNAL punishment " means punishment in that part of us which is eternal.

263.

TAKE a statement either as to the appearance of, or the audibility of the voice of a spiritual being, or as to that to which all other miracles may well be made subordinate—the power of raising from the dead. Surely if we cannot conceive the manner, we can, without any shock to our reason, comprehend it to be possible that the Almighty should cause matter to play round spirit, so that a broken or suspended connection may be resumed. This is not much more wonderful, though less common, than changes of matter with which we are familiar. Moreover with how many possible changes of matter we are not as yet familiar. If, for instance, all kinds of new lives can arise, which they clearly have done, out of the earth, or bright maggots out of a carcase, how much more naturally might the old lives rise out of their old mould again—especially if the type be not yet distributed, or the flesh be yet untainted, much more if it be yet warm! Of course this is answering a fool according to his folly. Who shall lay any

bounds to the tunes which the Divine
Music-master of the world can play upon
the notes of this dust of His? When
you look closely at your difficulty, it is the
alleged *rapidity* of the reported action of
the Almighty. If you believe in Him at
all, you know that He *can* do these things,
if you give Him time! But it is queer that
any man chymically given should think
the Eternal Chymist should require *time* for
His changes! He knows very well that
there is nothing in the nature of things to
prevent him and all his laboratory, and all
the workshop of the world from being hoist
about his ears "in a moment, in the twink-
ling of an eye." Nemesis drives these un-
divine diviners mad.

264.

HE managed his life and his Bible as
you see an ignorant or idle woman who is
searching for her route in a book of directions.
She has no fixed idea of how to find it.
She fumbles over the leaves upon false
clues, then listlessly and without any clue
at all, and at last she petulantly flings the

book aside. So he left off thought and
prayer, and flung aside the Book which,
carefully consulted and patiently searched,
had guided him safely through that laby-
rinth of life in which he is now likely to be
lost, losing all trains. Why does he not get
some discreet and learned minister to make
out his route for him?

265.

THERE may be various views of the
married relation, and there is literally but
an iota of difference, sometimes none at all,
between a *married* lot and a *marred* lot.
But with that view taken in the "Service for
the solemnisation of Matrimony," according
to which two people are regarded as "heirs
together of the Grace of Life," contrast the
following saying common among bachelor
bumpkins: "I arnt a gooin to give one
auf o moy food awaäy to get tother auf
cooked"! Yet who can blame these thrifty
men for not being willing to abandon a power
which flows from the reputed essence of
their humanity?

Phrygiæ
neque enim
Phryges—
V.

266.

In practical life, common-sense must temper logic, much as equity tempers justice. As equity is not better than justice, but is a better justice ; as casuistry is not better than moral law, but is in certain rare cases a better moral law ; so tact and practical wisdom are not better than logic, but are often a better logic.

267.

The ship a little sail can shift,
A slender tiller can persuade,
Not twenty stalwart hands can lift
On land—for which it was not made !

268.

. How speedily does what is called "a run of good luck" settle our minds into a condition of expecting its continuance. How soon do we cease to be thankful if it goes on, and begin to feel injured and to be disconcerted if it ceases ! Often a contented man, if a fortune be left to him, then for the first time in his life becomes a stingy grumbler.

269.

WE object to *pro*scribe religion, but we also object to *pre*scribe it. Thus, till we learn by experience that we must make up our minds what aspects of religion ought to be *pre*scribed, the whole of religion seems likely to be *pro*scribed and to go to the dogs of fanaticism ;—and the nation with it. For the State not yet to have found out that kernel in Christianity which is a *sine quâ non*, and which all serious people must admit, argues monstrous backwardness, betrays an ill eye to business, and bodes inconceivable calamity.

> You burn your spirits out with this wild anger. *Beau. & F.*

> You that guard virtue, are you asleep ? *Beau. & F.*

270.

WHEN people get somewhat old and the mind becomes flaccid, one of the difficulties of life lies in things getting lost or mixed : an invisible draught of circumstance seems to drift into confusion that infinity of small affairs from whose order ascends that subtle aroma called comfort. A wise man will look at this while he can, before he becomes ἀμαυρός.

> Velut ægri Somnia. *Hor.*

271.

IF in reading the thoughts and aspirations of a man like Wesley, or Joseph Hall, or Thomas à Kempis, I find any range into which I cannot as yet enter, I of course am at first disposed to set myself down as not yet having reached it, but to think it likely that I shall, if I follow on. I grant you must know your man before you can thus mistrust yourself while trusting *him;* but there are numberless men, whom, in their own mastered ranges of thought or feeling, you may come safely to trust.

272.

Two homes hath God from which He ne'er
      will part—
The highest Heaven, and the humble heart.

273.

THERE is no solitude so awfully oppressive as that which we feel in the noisy company of men who do not care to remember that the Father is with them. There is no social joy so exuberant as that of the soul who can pass lonely time in communing with God and being still.

Vengo in parte ove non e luca.
D.

"When evening was come, He was there alone."

274.

THE ravings, the unstrung babblings, the wayward ripplings of the dying Christian are worth a thousandfold more than the most calculated utterances of the burly man who is in all the insolence of health and in all the presumption of apparent sanity—but who is *wrong with God.*

275.

LORD Christ, what, where should I have been
    Had it not been for thee ?
And if Thou bide not by me still
    Where, what may I not be ?

276.

WESLEY'S hymns often end, like the voice of a man whose last reserve of emotion comes forth with an outburst, leaving the soul quiet and somewhat panting with faintness—as a racehorse after the dash of the finish ; or like the Voluntary of some great Musician, who draws out his thunder-stop before the Organ is still, so as to make the very walls of the Cathedral to shake, and the saints in the windows to tremble with pleasure.

Io pensai che l' Universo Sentisse amor. *D.*

277.

A FRIEND of mine, who does not profess to be fond of music, is only moved by music which is loud as well as good. Yet he is the last man who could be satisfied with *vox et præterea nihil.* I suppose he is shaken and trembles much as the walls and windows do, which are in no marked way touched by the tenderer passages. His material frame is affected. Yet morally he is the most tender of men, having the double-nature of the genuine poet and being the author of hymns, as well as histories, that must live. Of that best music he is himself a master.

" And let the base of Heaven's deep organ blow."
Milton.

278.

THERE is a mental and moral illusion akin to that experienced by the eye among objects in parallax. If we contemplate the progress of others, and the advance of opinion, and do not reflect upon our own position also, and our own relation to that opinion, we invert—that is, to our own perception—the order and movement of things.

Eppur si muove.

279.

TO A PARISIAN ACTRESS.

[*Who used after the play to carry her earnings for
the starving children of her* blanchisseuse, *whom,
without the knowledge of any one else, she nursed
through an illness.*]

THAT deed was gracious as the shower at night,
Which none have witnessed but the thoughtful
    sky,
The stars, and moon, if chance they caught
    the sight,
And the kind angels that were oaring by,
Heaven's couriers bent on kindred ministry;
For had not they attained their happy height
Because in love they took a long delight?
And shalt not thou be one with those on high?
The still shower stole into the garden's bosom,
The buds that hung a dying rose to blossom;
Nor till the morn could tell the Providence
Of that true dream of mute benevolence :—
Its gentle deed of loving-kindness done,
The shower stole back to heaven to meet the
    morning sun.

Rosa quo
locorum sera
moretur.
Hor.

280.

THE mind of the world, of an age, of a place, and of a man, may pass through many a perilous crisis : an obvious statement, but let it be noted and marked ; and let the crisis be watched for carefully, and steered through steadily. Some people seem to think that this question of State-Christianity is not one which for ever affects the English race, and therefore the type of Man :—νήπιοι. "Frustrate their politics, confound their knavish tricks : on Thee our hopes we fix ": God save the Defender of the Faith, and the Faith which hitherto She has defended, and which as yet She defends.

Sed si quid—ne quid—   *Ter.*

The angry spot doth glow on Cæsar's brow.   *Shaks.*

281.

SOCIETY, including books, is to the mind —and high society, including the highest Book, is to the soul—as food to the animal part.

282.

HE that, a pauper, takes a wife for pelf,
Is mostly one that only sells himself.

Il vero condito in—versi.   *D.*

283.

THE old tiger, thought to be dead, lifts up his right paw, and lays dead the man who approaches him from the left ; lifts up his left paw and floors dead the man who approaches him from the right, and then again himself seems as dead. So it is with many an old vice, both in the land and in the man.

284.

IT is clear that dark superstition has arisen, and must arise, from anchoring too habitually by the idea of the God of Power rather than by the God of Love ; by the physical God rather than by the moral ; by the Thunderer rather than by the Jesus— to Whom however all power is given in Heaven and on earth.

285.

REASON is as Faith's younger sister, and if rent from her side she soon must die ; and thus Faith be left alone to drag on a life that is but half a life, being one made up of contradictions and tears.

286.

THE persons confessedly best—by which I mean most trustworthy and respectable in the general estimate—best as friends and best as members of society, are those who really do as Christ bids them. Now take that fact, and ask whether a Christian is not therefore the kind of person for us to be? Can anybody upset that fact? Go to heathen or Mahommedan countries or to any human societies, and you will find that those who do the kind of things that Christ bids, whether they are conscious of it or not, are still the best. They do His will and know it not, but prosper in proportion as they do it. This being so, what are we to say of the Sovereign State which shall leave to chance influences the impressing of this character on its citizens? It might, as far as safety goes, leave it to the citizens if all were as some; but who can estimate the danger of neglecting the highest training of those masses who either learn Christ in some grotesque form, or not at all?

One is your MASTER, even CHRIST

Periculosæ plenum opus aleæ.
Hor.

Invalidique patrum referant jejunia nati.
V.

287.

"CULTURE" and "refinement" have their besetting vices, which no merely intellectual training will ever eradicate. The expression can be no truer of Culture than of Chivalry, that under its influence "vice itself loses half its evil by losing all its grossness." Rarely has so reckless a sacrifice as this been offered to an epigram. The essence of evil does not lie in its openness, but in its wrongness. If the *parade* of vice be part of its evil, then no doubt that part of it is lost when its voice is not heard in the streets ; but perhaps this is more than compensated by the additional allurements involved in the diminution of the chances of discovery.

288.

ETERNITY is not the Future, but rather the highest aspect of the unseen—future, present, and past—and is above the ideas of priority and posteriority. These ideas, and those which gather round them, vanish like meteors in the eternal sea.

A soul shall draw from out the vast, And strike his being into bounds.
Tenn.

289.

THE imagination, as well as the thoughts, are to be guarded from wandering. It requires a certain amount of deliberation and intention, to set the thoughts to plan and to arrange for, and to dwell distinctly on the best modes of compassing delights: but, even short of this, you must not allow the imagination to build up in the air of your soul, by the aid of bad memories, any unholy castles. You must not picture even remote possibilities, and fictitious contingencies ; for it may be moreover that these imaginations will some day become bodied forth. The Prince of the power of that air may some fine morning turn them to shape, and give to what seemed airy nothingness a name, an existence, and a local habitation— first in your thoughts, then in your acts, and at length in your habits. So your last end will be worse than your first. On this ground imagination is a " delusive faculty " *indeed.*

290.

TO THE MUSE OF PAINTING.

[Prefatory to poems from pictures.]

THOU of the poet-brush, I know
   Thy sister will not take it ill—
Thy sister, whose it is to glow
   With equal thought through painter-quill—

She will not look askant, to see
   That one, to her betrothed from youth,
Can cast some kindly looks on thee;
   Nor will she, can she, blame his truth.

If, listening to the poet's song,
   Thy chief of works thyself hast wrought,
How shall the poet work thee wrong
   To shape in words thy canvassed thought?

Yet hold me shriven that I presume
   To call thy spirit from its height;
Forgive me that my shallow plume
   Can hold but half thy pencil's light!

Tours, '51.

291.

THE surest way to Atheism is to act against or refuse to act upon the monitions of the conscience. If you refuse to acknowledge God personally, then you really acknowledge him nowhere. The ignoring of your own person, in your only personal region, namely your Conscience, which is the battle-ground of good and evil, naturally leads to, and in fact *is* the ignoring of the Personal Father of the Universe.

292.

WE know nothing yet as we ought to know, but we find reason to hope, that together with Christ we may go on living after we shall here be seen no more. Westcott's "Gospel of the Resurrection" indicates the line which must henceforth be taken by honest enquirers as to spiritual phenomena.

293.

EACH human act has a double bearing— one for time, and the other for eternity. An act, like the person who does it, is made up of spirit and matter.

294.

LET it be granted that the Spirit of God is Personal, and that He breathes forth and then breathes back the individual spirit of man. Why is man's spirit less personal when breathed back and after this life is over, than when breathed forth for this life to begin ? Is any man to say that a spirit cannot live in God because he knows not the ins and the outs of the modes of its future being? *This* life is *our* business : what business have we to puzzle ourselves as to other modes of existence, much less to dogmatise *against* it ? There is no dogmatism so positive as that of your negative dogmatist—" puppyism grown to maturity."

Lassa resedit * nec post oculis est reddita nostris.   *V.*

295.

WHATEVER else I know not, this I know,
That I am Thine, whether I stay or go.

296.

LET men beware lest in endeavouring to stop other mens' mouths they be haply found doing battle against the Head of the Church.

297.

OUR being out of spirits is mainly due to our not being " in the Spirit." Our being in bad spirits may be owing to bad spirits being in us, and may be best mended by bidding welcome to the good Spirit to dwell in us. Then we shall be more likely to be " in good spirits."

298.

WE cannot but observe that a seed of evil, a wrong idea, an undue regard, an unjust way of looking at some region of the life, once sown in the early nature, lives, abides and can germinate. It may be cut down ; it may remain buried out of sight, and seem to be wholly annihilated in the better growth of after years ; but there it is. And if the changes, the fortunes, the prosperities, or the calamities of life cause the opposite virtues to cease to flourish, and to have no further reason or scope for asserting themselves, then the character is sure to feel those old bad seeds and lurking weeds upon the stir, and often growing with frightful rapidity. Then if the man do not welcome

the Spirit of the sweet Saviour, and if he
do not stand upon the watch with rake and
hoe, spade and spud—the garden of the
Lord will soon be over-shadowed by the
rank luxuriance of sin.

299.

THY voice is the mere melody of thy heart :—
Those sightless chords (as some Æolian lyre,
That in confiding converse with the winds
Will render all the breath of heaven can bring)
Are set where dewy wafts of fragrant thought
Thrill through them from the garden of thy
 God
And lend them all they say.
 '52.

300.

WHEN "Jenny Lind" came to Oxford,
all my dear old tutor said was this : "She
has a woon-der-ful con-form-aation of the
laa-rynx." It was truly a most material
fact.

301.

A HOME of love will make a love of

302.

Indecoro
pulvere
sordidus.
Hor.

A MAN who does not clear his soul morn-ing and evening, and oftener, is like that careless man who has not placed, or does not use, the foot-scraper at his door. In this case he carries mud over all his chambers, in that he brings into all his doings something questionable and uncertain, which will need sweeping away.

303.

FAIR, as it fell, the morning snow
    Lies on you hills awhile,
Waiting to heaven again to go
    When once the sun shall smile.

So on my heart, this low-browed plot,
    Thy morning mercies lie;
But as my vulgar day grows hot,
    They vanish by and by.

But ah, henceforth, when ought comes down,
    May such good luck betide,
That I may make it all mine own,
    And lure it to abide.

Let me so praise Thee in my height,
    And reach Thee with my crest,
That all Thy graces that alight
    Grow parcel of my breast.

Sussex Downs, '76.

304.

THE Confessional may be abused in a thousand ways ; yet who that examines the idea can doubt the advantage of conscience-cleansing by aid of wise and good men ? Indeed, men who are gifted with spiritual insight, who love souls, and know in Whom they believe, are well known, whether they be clerical or lay—but especially if they be recognised as able Ministers of Christ's Church—to be mostly in the habit of assuring absolution to many who thus come to them—and to Jesus "by night."

Melioribus opto auspiciis.   V.

305.

NEVER think "how happy I could be if I might only break this or that commandment." That were indeed a most foolish and childish thought. Thou knowest not what thou thinkest.

Sequiturque Patrem non passibus æquis.   V.

306.

SINCE it is possible in words to confess God, and in works to deny Him, it may in some exceptional cases be possible in words to deny Him and in works to confess Him.

307.

SUCH mule-twist characters as are glanced at in the end of my last fragment, if "raised" in a Christian country probably owe to this fact that side of their nature which is for *confessing* God—that is, "in their works" or general conduct. To what then do they owe that side of their nature which uses God's gifts to *deny* Him before men?—But, let me ask by the way, *how* they deny Him? Why, in their "works"! So then we must limit the remark that they confess Him "in their works" to mean that they do so in *some* of their works; but not in those to which the name "works" is more expressly and significantly given, for we are now speaking of the prophets and prophetesses of literature. Charity, both theirs and ours, will cover the multitude of sins—but not *all*; nor can it (however many sins it may cover) mantle that positive mischief which is wrought in a sheep-like community by clever and charming, but Godless bell-wethers. As for charity, and general agreeableness, and open-handedness, *et id*

genus omne virtutum, I don't know any man
more given that way than a person who is
known to tread under foot some half-dozen
poor immortal dolls up and down the land,
and who is therefore no better, but worse
than the dead.—But I was asking to what
our mule-twist friends owe this God-deny-
ing side of their nature ? We find in their
shameless biographies (therefore there need
be no sort of delicacy in the matter) that
this is mainly due to the early neglect, un-
wisdom, or want of appreciation in fathers
and friends. Indeed they probably owe their
intellectual grit very much to that jarring
irritation of ungenial homes. I once said
to an Icenian serf, " How were you brought
up, Harry Mills ?" He gazed at me, with his
large blue eyes wide open, and with his jaw
dropped, and then said with a sardonic grin,
" Brawt oop?"—and here he broke into a
sorry laugh—"Brawt oop? wai, Sar, a *warnt*
brawt oop :—a wa *dragged* oop, kaind-o."
But this poor man suffered alone, and did
no harm in this distracted land ; for he was
not keen enough, nor imaginative enough,
and God had not given him force of genius

κᾆτα τίς
γαμεῖ ;
ἀλλ'
οἴκτισον
σφᾶς.
Soph.

enough to break through his wretched surroundings, and to avenge himself with reckless selfishness on his mother-country by
heading any crusade against the Cross. Indeed, I remember that, as I was minister-
ing to him (under my commission) in my
poor way, he came out with a pebble, which
I put into my pocket:—for he said "'Twan't
for hops, the heart ud braik," which being
interpreted meant, "The heart would break,
if it were not for hopes." (I am *quite* sure
that this last word is what he meant when
he said "hops," for poor Harry was not over-
fond of barley-broth !)

308.

WHAT ails thee, beautiful abele ? complain
Why thou alone art bent of all thy train;
I dare aver some unforgot mischance,
Unkind, in sapling days thee strook askance;
This having caught thee when of lowly length
" Grows with thy growth, and strengthens with
       thy strength ";
So keep thou wilt until thy latest leaf
The irreparable touch of that thine early grief.

309.

SET body, mind, and will in harmony,
To chaunt the parts of Life arranged by Thee.

310.

IT is but an ill compliment to the God of Truth to think that He cannot help us to fight His own battles without getting our falsehoods to help Him!

311.

THERE is a story of a man who fancied himself bigger than the doorway of the room in which he was ; he believed also that he was daily and hourly growing. His friends, assuring him that they traced no perceptible difference in his proportions, in vain urged him to put it to the proof by passing through the doorway. Smiling at so preposterous a proposal, he remarked that the result of so foolish an act on his part would be that his body and bones would be mangled into dissolution, in-evitable and immediate. They returned his smile, and amidst his groans and shrieks, dragged him from the apartment. Sure enough the poor wretch actually died. Now, whatever may be said of the wisdom of that mode of convincing him, did the result prove any the more that the man

τί γὰρ
ἐλλείπει
μὴ παρα-
παίειν ἡ
τοῦδε
τύχη;
Æsch.

τίς δ'
οἶδεν εἰ
ζῆν τοῦθ'
ὃ κέκληται
θανεῖν,
τὸ ζῆν δὲ
θνήσκειν
ἐστί.
Eur.

Men may
construe
things after
their fashion
Clean from
the purpose
of the things
themselves.
Shaks.

was what he thought he was? If his spirit thus squeezed out of him remains insane (which ghastly issue may God forefend!) he probably thinks he completely triumphed over his friends. It requires some care to put a thing to the test, and some wisdom to deduce conclusions therefrom!

312.

MUCH evil has arisen from the loose sense attached in common parlance to the word "idea." We speak of "a mere idea." But to the man of spiritual mind—that is, in point of fact—nothing can be more real than an idea, if it be in reality and not in phantasy.

313.

OH when at length, all phantasies offshaken,
When in Thy likeness shall I awaken?
The present, like a restless dream, have died
Along the edge of Being's darker side,
And I behold Thee, and be satisfied?

'52.

314.

A LITTLE *deference* saves a deal of *difference.*

315.

IF you wish to follow Paul's final advice, and think on things or persons pure, lovely, and of good report, dwell on those immortal Heroes of the Troubadours who took delight in love without desire. What an angelic contrast do they present to the bestial victims of desire without love !

Senza speme vivemo in disio. D.

316.

I KNOW a life much like an April day,
Here hung with clouds and there alive with
    sun ;
And neither in the selfsame mood will stay
While 'neath her heaven the winds of feeling
    run ;
Here all is dark where one short hour agone
Were thousand sunbeams lovingly at play ;
And presently, I trow, smiles many a one
Will chase the grief that now can lower so
    grey.
Such weather, to my mind, is fairer far
Than where the simmering hours all summer
    are :
Thy sorrow, girl, is more than duly sad,
But then thy gladness is divinely glad ;
And soon, methinks, a change will light thy
    brow,
And all thine hours be what the best are now.
    Heidelberg, '52.

ἔαρ
ὁρόωσα.
Theocr.

She had not learned the gamut yet of love.
    Fairfax.

317.

THERE is no great difficulty in roughly understanding instinct. It is only the draught of circumstance upon desire. What makes a dog go away from your house, and pursue its objects in the streets? You call it back—it cowers and comes! If you forget the beast and go off, the current of its allurement works again, and off it goes. The man who is nose-led by any desire can understand this, for he is precisely like that dog. So also can it be understood by the man, whom habit of prayer and of right action leads naturally and unconsciously to Church, to his favourite books of devotion, or to any good works. Instinct seems to include all those cases where the will does not distinctly interfere to guide action. The highest state of the soul is clearly where all the desires go right, being—as a matter of course, without effort, and even perhaps without discrete acts of judgment—under the guidance of the indwelling Spirit. When the soul becomes thus instinctively right in its movements, the will becomes quite subject to Him that before put some things under it, that God may be all in all. It becomes one with God's will, and saving identity, at one with God. Thus man at his best comes round to the inner condition of the dog, which God also made, and said was, in its type, very good. Man would have been as good as the dog at first, but for the will. If his will does not rise into instinctive repose in God's will, his last state is worse than the brute's first.

ἐπ' ἔσχα-τα βαί-νεις. Soph.

318.
THE State that abandons Christianity to random and individual efforts, ceases to be Sovereign.

Prudens pravè.

319.
DEAR Church, the belfry of your mind
Is weaker than the hymns you sing;
The sway of those great thoughts, you find,
Rocks your frail Temple while they ring.

320.
THE only real lights of the world are holy souls. Miss Porter somewhere says, "The only lights of the city were the tapers by the shrines of the saints."

Let your light so shine. CHRIST.

321.

IT may fairly be asked whether, had we always been good hitherto, we should not always have the witness of the Spirit now? May not the broken character of our communications from above be due to the broken character of our earlier lives? It would seem to follow of necessity that some such result should arise from all the irregularities of our boyhood and youth, the greater if they were greater, the less if they were less, but all in measure due. Was *nothing* to follow from all those pieces of duties left undone, from all those voices and monitions of conscience silenced or satisfied but ill? from all those prayers hurried over, which for the most part were *not* prayers? from all those permitted discontents and ambitions—not to name evils possibly worse than these? Has our soul to bear no scars for all this? We must indeed be suffering for it. And is not this the mode in which the penalty comes, namely, in the not being spoken to by God so regularly and unbrokenly as His longer and more intimate worshippers? Aye,

μὴ οὐκ ἔχων τι σύμβο-λον.
Soph.

even still, who can tell how oft he offend-
eth? oh cleanse thou us from our secret
faults. Efface the scars of the past, heal
the wounds that rankle now, through our
future keep us whole, and after all bring us
to the blessed days in the land of promise.

322.

ARE all these men, who provide the ne-
cessaries and dainties which you pay for, to
find solid happiness in work and industry,
and are *you*, because you have the blessing
of being born "a gentleman," to get your
only satisfaction by the sweat of other
men's brows? Nothing of the sort, my
friend. St. Paul says, "Except a man work,
neither shall he eat:" that is, you cannot
have wholesome enjoyment and good di-
gestion without *some* kind of labour. Your
very pleasures must be laboriously ordered
to last pleasant for long.

323.

THE Queen ceases to be Sovereign in the
highest sense, if she ceases to teach CHRIST
to her people.

ἄλει,
μύλα,
ἄλει.
Old Song.

Exercere
diem.
V.

324.

WHY is it that we are naturally disposed to waive the direct mention of the person in whom we are most interested—sometimes, which is most singular, even by using the plural ? " I hope the same parties is doing the garding," wrote a lady's-maid to a fellow-servant, of course in the postscript— " parties " in this case meaning her single *amoròso*.

*   *   *   *   *   *

In Mrs Poyser's part of the country it seems to be the habit to speak of the Supreme Being as "They," and that without intending Polytheism—much less any special Church doctrine. We like to keep a kind of precinct round our innermost lives, within which hardly anybody is to approach without taking off the shoes. The whole question of Reserve goes very deep and repays examination.

325.

YOU are ill able to bear a mere *nothing*, if your conscience is ill at ease : but you are well able to bear almost *anything* if your conscience is easy.

326.

"YE see me." Bp. Berkeley denied truth in seen form. CHRIST affirms truth of unseen Spirit. That negation, however, is a correlative of this affirmation. Berkeley said that is not which you see. CHRIST says "That is which you see not"; nay, sublimating the intuition, He says, "You see that Unseen which is." As in the word Jehovah, so in Christ's expression "Ye see me," past, present, and future are wound in one to make a garland for the Church's Head—Jesus Christ, the same yesterday, to-day, and for ever. Very like this is "Lo, I am with you *always*." He says "Before Abraham was, I *am*"; and again "The Son of Man who *is in Heaven*." The statement "ye see me,"—which might almost seem at first to be a loose expression or else a figure, for which "ye *shall* see me" might as well have been substituted—is really but an eternal fusing of posteriority and priority in Christ's assertion of His spiritually visible presence. It is "the future in the instant," the instant attracted on to the future—or rather, the fine brush of the Divine word is

Yet a little while, and the world shall see me no more; but ye see me. John xiv. 19.

N

drawn over the adjacent tints of time, so as to heighten their interest and beauty, while it blends them all with an eternal air, and tones them into harmony.

327.

WHEN the gentle delicacy of thought and the clear language of fine intuition sink and become lost to us in an unexpressive haze of sound; when the sweetness of the smile that we knew passes into looks that we know not; when "decay with its defacing fingers hath swept the lines where beauty lingers"—so that we turn away from the forms even of the most loved, the most good, and the most beautiful ; and when we see them borne away into the dark lap of the earth—what is it but that a cloud receives him, or a cloud receives her, out of our sight ? Yet happily the cloud which thus overshadows the beloved sons and daughters of God—both when they see their loved ones enter into it, and when they enter into it themselves—is a bright one, out of which comes the Father's voice. This being so, why need we fear ?

οὐ φιλάν
ἀλλὰ
φιλτάταν.
Eur.

328.

FAITH is but Reason in her attitude of love ; Reason is but Faith in her moments of reflection.

Tendebat-
que manus
ripæ ulteri-
oris amore.
V.

329.

*[To his love, whose forehead had been scarred by the
fall of an hour-glass.]*

As one who feels the rossignol
Regale the listening grove with song,
And well the fulness of her soul
In measured torrent all night long,

So I with thee, love, by my side :
Such harmony of heart redounds,
I dance upon my life's high-tide,
And all my day runs diamonds.

ἐνθ' ἀ
λίγεια
μινύρεται
ἀηδὼν
ἀνέχουσα
τὰν ἄβα-
τον θεοῦ
φυλλάδα.
Soph.

Time had not dropped that sorry glass,
Nor found the heart to wound thy brow,
Hadst thou but taught him then to pass
The hours that thou hast taught him now.

Te, tuumque
dulce caput.
V.

Or knew he what should come to us ?
So, fretful at his hopeless task,
Poor petulance, defaced thee thus,
Full loth to grant what love should ask ?

He felt thy life could laugh to scorn
The lobes in that his palsied hand;
That there was something to be born
Would need no more his grains of sand.

Ah yes! the green-eyed dotard knew
When first he saw thee in thy prime,
A love should run between us two,
Which should not thank the count of time.

Nor yet would all the shores of earth
Mete any measure for the love,
That, breaking forth in better birth, ·
Would prove itself immense above.

So Time may chafe, and Time may rail,
And Time's last glass in shivers lie,
While thou and I crowd snowy sail
Across the free Eternity.

    Brussels, '52.

Indocilis
pauperiem
pati. *Hor.*

ἆρ' εὐτυ-
χεῖς οὖν
τοῖς γά-
μοις, ἤ
δυσ-
τυχεῖς;
   Soph.

330.

LIFE is apt, with most people, to run rather low when lacking a fair share of love: but then such people must only the more closely cultivate the love of "The Invisible."

331.

THE love of pleasure spoils the pleasure of love.

332.

IN all our contests, outward and inward, we must take care to keep our ears open to the lightest whisper of that Voice behind us. We must not go on in advance beyond the guidance of that Voice. There are many things which we had better not think of now. We shall, if we endure to the end, have powers and leisure to enter upon many speculations, when our Heavenly Father shall let us walk in a happy Eternity beside the river of the water of life; and so let us lay aside such contemplations till then.

ὅμοια
ὁμοίοις
γινώσκε-
ται.

333.

THERE are two modes of tenure, one *on* earth and the other *in* earth. One is the way in which we hold land, the other the way in which land holds us.

ἔστιν δὲ
τῆς ἐμῆς
χθονὸς
λαχεῖν
τοσοῦτον,
ἐνθανεῖν
μόνον.
Soph.

334.

A WEAK believer is timid in proportion to the weakness of his belief.

Hoc fit ubi
non verè
vivitur.
Ter.

στάσιν
γλώσσης.
Soph.

ψεύδεα
πολλὰ
λέγων,
ἐτυμοῖσιν
ὁμοῖα.
Hom.

335.

IT is very important to observe how close an analogy subsists between the position of the ancient Jewish Church as the people of the Father-God, and that of the Christian Church as the people of the Son-God. The parallel is trite and obvious, but in the following respect I think it is often forgotten. Indeed I have never, that I remember, seen it noticed. But that is probably a part of my ignorance. At any rate, let me put the argument as it strikes me. Some sectarians, though I believe the number is on the decline, think—and "teach men so,"—that our standing as a Christian nation is nothing; that the practice of universal baptism is a mistake; that we should wait for individual conversion; that persons can in no respect be regarded as Christians till they become so far adult as to be able to make a conscious and public profession!

It may be said in passing, that no one, in all the centuries of that great Church which at a precious cost has handed down to us all the Truth which we have to live upon, had ever ventured to put forth this idea till

about two centuries ago—except Montanus.
Him all the Church—and that, take note,
before its corruption—regarded as a "here-
tic," that is, a man who chose the questionable course of setting up his own opinion
against that of all Christendom. On the later
parentage of Anabaptist views it does not
concern me here to dwell. Suffice it to say
that it was not a likely stock to produce
any very valuable revolution in religious
thought.

But I would now only make bold to
ask those who make it a matter of conscience to maintain these unsettling theories,
to mark and inwardly digest the following
fact. Although there was of course always a
deep distinction between the common Israelite and the "Israelite indeed, in whom there
was no guile," yet *all the Jews were regarded
by the prophets as the chosen people. God addresses them, without exception, as "my people."*
Those were called even "gods" to whom the
Word of God came, in mere virtue of God's
Word having come to them ; and, as Christ
Himself adds, "The Scriptures cannot be
broken." In keeping with this, Stephen

addresses his very murderers as his "breth-ren and fathers." Now I would ask my Baptist friends whether they do not think that those to whom the Word of *Christ* has come—and who have received, in virtue of their being children of a Christian nation, the sign of infant baptism, which Christ Himself ordained as the outward mark of His people—may, in mere virtue of Christ's Word having come to them, be much more called Christians and regarded as Chris-tians?

Let me add that what I have here said shows the folly either of thinking infant baptism enough, or of counting it for nothing.

336.

AN old disused clock was standing on my mantel-shelf. A friend enquired, "What's the time?" looked at his own watch, and at my clock, and said, "Your clock is *exactly* right." I said "Yes, you have con-sulted it exactly at one of the only two occasions in the twenty-four hours when it *is* right : for now, though it is a lucky hypocrite, it does not go ! " What credit we sometimes get by lucky hits. " No wonder," said my friend, " it holds its hands before its face."

337.

A PHILOSOPHICAL friend said to me the other day, " If I am sent to such and such a work, it will be an appointment. If not it will not be a *dis*appointment, but simply a *non*-appointment."

They also serve who only stand and wait. *Milt.*

338.

IF you leave the light of God you become the victim of some form of superstition. If you become the victim of any form of superstition, you are so far out of the light of God. Even England is full of super-stition, among its many remnants of pagan-ism. You can hardly find a person,—nay, a parson—who does not on the sly cap a magpie ! In the " best " families, even in this advanced land, superstitions are trans-mitted by nurses. What a field for Rome !

About him fairies sing a scornful rhyme, And as you trip him, pinch him to your time. *Shaks.*

339.

So important is the special and individual play of the Christ-Spirit in each person's nature, that, if every man and woman were exactly to imitate Christ's mode of life, society obviously could not go on for a year. Those books which run down modern Christianity because Christians do not follow the details of Christ's modes of life, clearly have a mental twist. This it is which mainly accounts for their being read.

340.

An *aimless* life is commonly a *nameless* life.

341.

How mysterious is all hidden life, and how pleasant to ponder. There is manifold sweetness in the mingled odour of a garden or a field, which only unfolds its beautiful and subtle sources to the attentive nerves.

There is deep interest in the confused murmur of birds, bees, breezes, voices, and sheepbells, which only unravels itself to the leaning and listening ear.

There is a wonderful infinity in far shadows, and also in the multitudinous life of a peopled landscape which only unveils its forms to the studious eye.

So, if you are flung into a society, as that of a City or Town, that which at first may seem common and unclean will reveal itself in a beautiful order and present distinct phenomena, if, under the Divine influence of grace and love, you will regard humankind with a kindly humanity.

There is untold depth in the sayings of the wise, especially of the All-Wise, which only unfathoms itself to the pondering spirit. What wonderful life we may find hidden with Christ in God!

Juvat integros accedere fontes.
V.

Verba Verbi.

342.

THOSE who do not step forward, and fill up, and grow into God in all things—will fall back, and shrivel up, and grow down into the devil in all things.

We may be "in the Kingdom" and yet "the Kingdom" may not be *in us*.

αἱ δὲ τοιαῦται φύσεις αὐταῖς δικαίως εἰσὶν ἄλγισται φέρειν.
Soph.

343.

He wrote gold stars on yonder round blue
     wall
That rings horizons-full of loveliness;
He breathed the laws of life and crowned them
     all
In breathing one who should them all possess;
It was His pleasure from His store to call
Whatever most this living soul might bless;
We, made with choice to stand, made choice to
     fall—
Yet even so doth Heaven regard us less?
Nay, with a patient sorrow all the while,
He lets us feel a sunshine in His smile;
He fills our hearts with gladness, and for food
With daily dole delights to do us good :—
Oh how would Earth and Man run o'er with
     beauty,
If, as He holds to Love, we held to Duty.

Frankfort, '52.

344.

WHAT a sensation of buoyancy you feel when you stand on a pier at the moment when the spring-tide is at the height of the gladness of its gallop past the posts at the mouth of a river. High-busy in the impetuosity of its career—standing to matter something as Time does to mind, and like Time, its co-factor and twin-brother in the planet—it waits for no man, while every man that wants it must wait for it. Up it gathers, rounding its bright back in mid-channel. Bound upon bound it lifts itself to master and swallow the land ; the more if urged and chased by the after-play of some South-wind that it has left lagging in the lurch, and that works upon it far in the rear. What excitement it raises in the inhabitants of the place who come to watch it ! Little children run from it with screams mingled with delight, while heavily-moving men—who before, like Spaniards, felt too dignified to run—now with sodden shoon and shining raiment skip aside grotesquely nimble. What sudden replenishing of hollows, what rushing up into creeks, what pouring in mimic falls through all openings, and what oozing and weltering through crevices! What reboant multitudinous exultation now is everywhere. But how can any-one—except a Ruskin—describe this picture? See it again writhing its refulgent neck, coil after coil making its way to its object with swiftness incredible and irresistible. The marvel is that ever it comes to a stop. In a field of race-horses, as over yonder on the Ducal Down of Goodwood, you can follow somewhat more fixedly the twinkle and glitter of their gallop, and the flash of their shining flanks, as they sweep, huddled in one stream, to the winning post; but, as with the motion of some vast boa-constrictor, this infinite sea in its racings—having no special limbs and parts in which we can notice its progress, because it is swayed by undulation rather than motion—seems to move the more magnificently because every particle of it seems to move at once and coherently. Like the cloud of the poet, " It moveth all together if it moves at all."

πᾶς γὰρ ἀστράπτει χαλινὸς πᾶσα δ' ὁρμᾶται πώλων ἄμβασις.
Soph.

ἵππους, ἄγαλμα τῆς ὑπερπλούτου χλιδῆς.
Æsch.

345.

REACTION is commonly only another name for *in*action.

Vom Regen in die Traufe.

346.

THE day was as calm as summer could make it. It was only when you held the sound of the breaking of your own breath on your lips that you heard the little pretences of waves playfully patting the sand with a lap-lap-sough, sough-sough-lap. A flight of ox-birds rose close by, and in faith the whirring of their little wings was more effective and outspoken than the breaking on the long low shore of all the waters of the potential Channel.

εὖτε πόν-
τος ἐν
μεσημ-
βριναῖς
κοίταις
ἀκύμων
νηνέμοις
εὖδοι
πεσών.
Æsch.

347.

WHAT is *auricular* we are sometimes disposed to feel may be *oracular*.

348.

A MAN who is removed from frequent converse with congenial minds must be on his guard lest not only his thoughts perish, but his power of thinking and expressing himself, be those powers great or small, perish likewise. If those powers be small, it is only the more important, to him at least, that they should survive ; for they enter into the essence of his eternity. Most people are ἀνθρωπολόγοι, and when the doings and sayings of men become elevated, these will form an interesting topic of conversation ; but at this stage of ordinary society the topic is mostly depressing, if dwelt upon unduly. This being so, a man who finds that the matter of life has set over against it in his soul a love of contemplating its relations, must talk to something, if not to some one ; or he will lower his capacity and lose an integral portion of the organic structure of his being. Self-preservation is a leading law of spiritual and mental as well as of material nature. What reasonable hope has a man of recovering that which he thus loses ? A plant when neglected in its thumb-pot will never be that which it otherwise might have been. Therefore he must make a companion of his pocket-books, like Lucilius :—

En sola voluptas solamenque mali.   *V.*

Ille velut fidis arcana sodalibus olim
Credebat libris, neque si malè cesserat unquam
Decurrens alio, neque si bene; quo fit ut omnis
Votivâ pateat veluti descripta tabellâ
Vita senis.

If some partial friend should come and pick
his pocket or make him rake it out and stand
and deliver some of his unpolished gatherings, it is him that my gentle public must
thank if they dislike them. So let your poor
pebble-man pass along his beach as before,
and grant him the verdict, "Not guilty, and
we hope will never do it again." On the
other hand, should the publisher, his old
and valued friend of thirty years,—even in
the days of his brother Daniel, that man
of "excellent spirit"—should Alexander
Macmillan see cause to ask for more, the
pebble-man can only say, in Lincolnshire
phrase, "Theer's plenty more wheer them
coom fra."

πάντες
ἀγαπῶσι
μᾶλλον
τὰ αὑτων
ἔργα,
ὥσπερ οἱ
γονεῖς καὶ
οἱ ποιηταί
Ar.

Sequor et
quâ ducitis
adsum.
V.

349.

How slight a touch can give spirit and
force to a rendering. I recollect, as boys at
Rugby, we were preparing the first Book of

the Histories of Tacitus with that beloved
Tutor, who was afterwards Bishop of Cal-
cutta. One of us, carried away by the indignant stream of his author, was translating
that 40th chapter, in which is pictured the
miserable end of Galba—" Igitur Romani
milites, quasi Vologesen aut Pacorum avito
Arsacidarum solio depulsuri, ac non Im-
peratorem suum inermen et senem truci-
dare pergerent, &c." We had been all
stirred by the manner in which E. H. S.
gave the former part of the chapter; but
most of all when he said, " soldiers, and
they Roman soldiers, not as if they were
going to butcher an old and unarmed man
—their own Emperor—but as if they were
about to drive a Vologeses or a Pacorus
from the ancestral throne of the Arsacidæ."
—I well remember how the throwing in of
that little indefinite article before those two
proper names brought a subdued applause
from poor Cotton, and from all the listening
Fifth.—It may not be uninteresting to
mention by the way that the above rendering was given by one who can now command applause from a listening Senate;

and who, in defence of Christian nationali-
ties, translating the spirit of the English
people, would, if the moral force put forth
were to prove insufficient, do everything,
*excepting always any act unstatesman-like or
un-English*, to drive from the ancestral
Throne of the Ottomans an Abdul that is,
or an Abdul that shall be, or whatever name
may be borne by his Sultanic Majesty.—
But I only meant to show what the happy
throwing in of the letter "a" did for that
sentence.

Non defen-
sonibus istis
Tempus eget
V.

Let onion
atoms lurk
within the
bowl,
And scarce
suspected
animate the
whole.
Syd. Smith.

350.

No man was intended to lose his originality, much less to go mad upon it. The
preservation of balanced peculiarity in the
character of our spirit and our mind is
essential to a deep sanity.

351.

WHAT *is* a fault, confess at once and flee from,
But never own a fault that thou art free from.

Let no man
take thy
crown.

352.

THERE is one heresy graver than Ration-
alism; and that is *Irrationalism !*

353.

ALWAYS try to remain in the attitude in which you are when you make your best prayers. Moses' face shone *after* he came down from the mount.

354.

OH good and virtuous, kindly and charitable unbeliever, who sittest at Christ's table and breathest the air and eatest of the good things of this Christian Society, but who yet givest the lie to the Governour of the Feast, does not *this* seem to you a thing to be noted ? that, however good you may think you are, and however independent you may make yourself of God and His Son, and of prayer and holy ways, yet that all these very states are exactly those to which all people come when they are bad, and when they leave off being good ? Bad people—I mean people who are exactly opposite to the salt of the earth, people by whom society (which you appear to wish to preserve) is being decayed and broken up and drawn away from all sound and conservative principle—all such persons have it for their main characteristic that they run down our blessed Saviour, or at least tread his salvation under foot, just as you do. Is not that a *sign*, if not a *proof*, that you are in the wrong boat? and that it would be wise for you to set about going up a little closer to Christ? Ask Him who He is, and what He means. You might possibly get a little light from a fragment of reflection on this head.

Lord, to whom shall we go? Thou hast the words of eternal life. —John vi. 68

355.

ARE we now far from India? or are we near? What is distance reckoned by? by our bodies being carried? or by communication of our minds and spirits? If by the latter, we are near. This question is interesting as bearing on things which are not seen, but which are eternal. We were a long time before we could transfer our minds and spirits to distant peoples, and do great works afar off by a word. The inhabitants of an Indian village see vast railway works suddenly set afoot; a flash of verbal lightning from England did it. This is as singular to them as it is to unspiritual men to find it said that diseases fled at the word of Christ, that the veil of the Temple and the rocks were rent, and that the bodies of the Saints showed themselves in the Holy City. This too was at the will of an unseen Power. We have not yet learned the hidden causes and means which may thus be set in motion by that mysterious Invisible Personal Cause whom most of us recognise. Can anybody who regards the growth of knowledge suppose that we have stood as far from God all this time as He has seemed in our unconsciousness to stand from us? The interest of life largely consists in the fact that the atmosphere of mind and spirit is alive with uncaught ideas. Would it not be more philosophical if, instead of going into the region of the Christian records with hard and closed heart and eyes, we were to wait awhile in humble faith and with open truth-desiring eyes, till we learn somewhat more of the rationale of spiritual telegraphy?

Though He be not far from every one of us.
St. Paul.

356.

THE more well-to-do you are, the more bound you are to do well.

357.

WHERE is to be the limit to our forgiv-
ingness ? Our prayer is, "Forgive us, as
we forgive." If there is to be a limit to our
forgiving, there must be a limit to our
being forgiven ! Who will not here say,
"God forbid"? If God can forgive a forgiving soul all manner of sin and blasphemy
but that which is "against the Holy Ghost,"
which however no forgiving soul can commit,
what limit can we poor mortals place to our
power of forgiving? What care we should
take that we lead no one who in any way
depends upon us to despair of our forgiving
him. With what humble readiness should
we spring forward to assure him that such
a state of mind towards him would to us
miserable sinners be impossible. With
what thoughtful delicacy should we distinguish and discriminate the phases and
degrees of error, and even crime. How
should we guard our weak fibre from being
driven by fret and frenzy into blundering
and wholesale denunciation, and curb that
noblest indignation which may plunge into
words never to be unsaid, if not into deeds

never to be undone. And you will be able to blame with the more healing effect, if you can pick out even some little point for praise. You must make it manifest that, loving the person to be blamed, it is the sin, and only the particular sin, which you then discountenance. If your brother knows his Saviour, your course is comparatively easy. If he does not know his Saviour, it is the Saviour that you must bring him to know. Your love must be without dissimulation, that is, as plain and outspoken as you can find, or make, scope for. Find fault only where you must, and make happy all you can. In your power and manner of doing this lies your utility as a minister or a handmaid of the sweet Master. Samuel Wilberforce used to say to his candidates for ordination, "Sympathy must be your golden key."

A heart at leisure from itself, To soothe and sympathise.
Anna L. Waring.

358.

THE unchecked enjoyment of the desires of the mind, like the unchecked enjoyment of those of the body, is a folly and a sin, and leads to ruin and corruption. Mental action may doubtless serve to keep down and supplant still lower motions of the life; I mean, the mere phytic or sensual impulses, as the excesses of the pleasures of touch, taste, and the like : but the mental motions themselves can only be kept from running riot, and from becoming ruinous in their own ranges, by our walking "*in the Spirit.*" Thus alone can we avoid fulfilling the desires of the mind as well as of the flesh. I hardly know anything more important in morals than to acknowledge this tripartite division of the composite man. To those who do not, the colours of humanity, as with an artist who is but a tyro, run, and their harmony is lost in a muddy confusion.

Here the Priest shall make a cross upon the child's forehead.
Rubric.

359.

To the GOD-MAN.

So closely art Thou in God's heart,
 And God so close in Thine,
I marvel which is human part
 And which is Thy divine.

Thou, Father, art in me, and I in Thee.—John xvii. 21

360.

PROCRASTINATION is the thief of——

Behold now is the accepted time ; behold now is the day of

salvation.—
2 Cor. vi. 2.
While it is
called To-
day.—Heb.
iii. 13.

ETERNITY.

361.

IN the relation of wind to flame there is a point of very critical moment, no less than this :—whether the breath of the air be such as to invigorate or to annihilate, to silence the little fiery tongue into blackness of darkness, or else blow it into blaze. Look at the tenderness of the Divine Spirit: "He will not quench the smoking flax."

It sat upon
each of
them.—Acts
ii. 3.

362.

You had not deemed so cold a mien
Could ere have kindled so ;—
And yet the sunlight may be seen
Less lovely on the summer green
Than on a lawn of snow.

363.

THERE are two reasons, among others, why some men love darkness rather than light ; lest they see the public and private enormity of their sin, and lest they see the outer and inner consequences of it. Were they to see either one or the other, they would not feel able to enjoy it. Of course all reasons are shut up in that one which the Master gives.

Because their deeds are evil.

364.

CONSIDERING our advantages, and to most of my readers I may add, considering our age, where ought we not now to be on our Christian course ? What evil tendency ought we not by now to have mastered ?

Ah ! what avails superior light Without superior love ? *Wes.*

365.

I THINK the meekest thing, and at the same time the most ironical thing, which Christ ever said, is recorded by St. John, chapter 8. " I have not a devil."

Out of His mouth went a sharp two-edged sword. —Rev. i. 16.

366.

IT is a good thing when you perform the solemn act of winding up your watch— whose chain may run longer than your own —to pray.

Ineluctabile tempus. *V.*

367.

SOMETIMES when a preference is given on the ground that a case is more *urgent*, it only means that the case has been more *urged*.

ἔστι τοῦ λέγοντος· *Soph.* τὸ δ' ἀξίωμα κ.τ.λ. *Eur. Hec.*293

368.

Night-prayer by the Sea.

KING of the vasty water-floods of grace,
With Thee I pace beside Thy waves to-night—
My barren spirit, like this foot-marked place,
Crossed and recrossed by thoughts that were
       not right.
O may an even, washed, and ordered space
Meet the new visit of the Day-star bright;
To-morrow may no wandering sin leave trace
On that clear level left at morning light.
And hear me, heavenly Spirit, when I pray
Thy boundless Love to lave me day by day;
May no unsightly flotson lig, and bide
The sweeping refluence of Thy nightly tide;
Here, Father, let me love with Thee to walk,
And ever feel Thee smile and hear Thee talk.

Littlehampton, '69.

369.

IT is odd that in the great prayer-hymn which Bishop Ken made for us, and in which the English people sing the invocation to their souls to awake, we compare ourselves to a stager—an old coach-horse. I suppose this is why modern editors have lost the lively image in the common word 'course:' but, however absurd it may be to sing it, the people have hitherto been content to be likened unto a poster.

ὥσπερ ἵππος εὐγενής. *Old Play.*

370.

HOW the results of a dead man's spirit can be vigorous and visible—how succeeding generations can feel with a man, love a man, bless a man, or possibly entertain uncomfortable feelings about a man—and yet how the spirit of that man can be without any form of life, is a thing which those must explain who deny it. Aristotle's idea that these events penetrated to the dead in some faint way may be true enough, though it was probably a piece of humorous dealing with an impenetrable difficulty. Perhaps voices *to* the grave are as thin, as voices

ὧν ἔρως φύσει ἐστίν. *Ar.*

from the grave? The master of pre-Christian knowledge felt, however, unable to deny that the spirits of men live hereafter. Be it noted also that, however thin the *voices* may be supposed to be, **this does** not involve any opinion of emaciation in the after-life of the individual from whom, or to whom they may come. The vocal obesity may depend on the medium and interval of passage.

371.

Music sleeps in the plain egg.
Tenn.

I SING because I am,
   I am because I sing ;
If life or song the sooner came
   Is past conceptioning.

372.

Inscription for the Register of Burials.

MAY all who breathe this mortal breath
   And strive this mortal strife,
Ere written in our book of death
   Stand in Thy Book of Life.

373.

Pro re pauca loquar.
V.

LET your going out and coming in be with humility, respect, and grace. Often shut to the door and confront yourself with

the Master-Builder of your life and the
Architect of the world. Be able to lay
your hand on your breast and on the Book,
and to call down a blessing on your guileless resolution. Act on the square ; be
what they call in Lincolnshire a " level "
man ; rectify your walk by the plummet of
truth ; observe all your relations with all
your brethren, and measure them with the
compasses of a sound judgment ; observe
strict morals ; let brotherly love continue ;
relieve to the best of your ability those with
whom, in the course of your time, you are
brought into more especial brotherhood ;
and let these virtues distinguish you
through all the grades of your ascent
through life. This will be to live always
in the noonday. You will thus show signs
of always being with your Master ; you will
give tokens of keeping the best company ;
your words will be seasoned with signifi-
cant grace ; and you will so pass pleasantly
into that prepared and abiding Building of
God—the House not made with hands,
eternal in the Heavens.

374.

1 John iv. 21

NOT till I loved Thee did I know Thee, nor till I knew Thee did I love Thee. I loved Thee at first under the hazy veils of a faith that was but half-faith ; but when I came to know even what I know of Thee now, the love I had before seemed un-meet to be called love, and yet it was that which lured me on to know Thee, and so to love Thee, more. Nor even yet doth mine eye nearly see Thee as Thou art.

Till Thou
my patient
spirit guide
Into Thy
perfect love.
Wes.

375.

LOVE broadens, lengthens life ; below, above, Who loves the most to live will live the most to Love.

ἐγὼ δ'
ὔμμιν καὶ
ἐς ὔστερον
ἅδιον ᾀσῶ
Theocr.

'ΑΦΙΣΤΑΜΑΙ.

ROBERTS, PRINTER, BOSTON, LINCOLNSHIRE.